THE COLD WAR CHRONICLES

Nuclear Proliferation, the Military-Industrial Complex, and the Arms Race

Kaitlyn Duling

Cavendish Square
New York

Published in 2018 by Cavendish Square Publishing, LLC
243 5th Avenue, Suite 136, New York, NY 10016

First Edition

Library of Congress Cataloging-in-Publication Data

Names: Duling, Kaitlyn.
Title: Nuclear proliferation, the military-industrial complex, and the arms race / Kaitlyn Duling.
Description: New York : Cavendish Square, 2018. | Series: The Cold War chronicles | Includes index.
Identifiers: ISBN 9781502627308 (library bound) | ISBN 9781502627247 (ebook)
Subjects: LCSH: Nuclear nonproliferation--Juvenile literature. | Nuclear weapons--Juvenile literature. | Cold War--Juvenile literature. | Arms race--Juvenile literature.
Classification: LCC JZ5675.D85 2018 | DDC 327.1'747--dc23

Editorial Director: David McNamara
Editor: Jodyanne Benson
Copy Editor: Rebecca Rohan
Associate Art Director: Amy Greenan
Designer: Alan Sliwinski
Production Coordinator: Karol Szymczuk
Photo Research: J8 Media

The photographs in this book are used by permission and through the courtesy of: Cover Roger Viollet/Hulton Archive/Getty Images; p. 4 Aviation History Collection/Alamy Stock Photo; p. 10 U.S. Federal Government/ Wikimedia Commons/File:Manhattan Project emblem.png/Public Domain; p. 14 The National Archives, United Kingdom/Wikimedia Commons/File:Yalta Conference 1945 Churchill, Stalin, Roosevelt.jpg/Public Domain; p. 17 US Army/Wikimedia Commons/File:Firestorm cloud over Hiroshima.jpg/Public Domain; p. 19 Nicholas Kamm/ AFP/Getty Images; p. 22 US Government/Wikimedia Commons/File:Double sentence-spaced typewriter text vs. singlespaced printed text - vertical comparison.jpg/Public Domain; p. 26 MPI/Archive Photos/Getty Images; p. 28 Daily Mirror/Mirrorpix/Getty Images; p. 32-33 SSPL/Getty Images; p. 35 Underwood Archives/Archive Photos/ Getty Images; p. 38, 73 Bettmann/Getty Images; p. 41 Dominick Reuter/AFP/Getty Images; p. 43 SDASM Archives (https://www.flickr.com/people/49487266@N07)/Wikimedia Commons/File:Atlas ICBM Launch--'(no text on envelope or negative) (15908372710).jpg/Commons; p. 48, 63 Corbis/Getty Images; p. 53 Everett Collection Inc./ Alamy Stock Photo; p. 56 George Skadding/The LIFE Picture Collection/Getty Images; p. 59 Julian Wasser/ The LIFE Images Collection/Getty Images; p. 65 Fine Art Images/Heritage Images/Getty Images; p. 70 National Archives/Wikimedia Commons/File:Cuban missiles.jpg/Public Domain; p. 76 TASS/Getty Images; p. 79 NSSDC, NASA/Wikimedia Commons/File:Sputnik asm.jpg/Public Domain; p. 81 Alex Dellow/Picture Post/Getty Images; p. 84 Pallava Bagla/Corbis/Getty Images; p. 87 Encyclopedia Britannica/UIG/Getty Images; p. 90-91 Universal History Archive/UIG/Getty Images; p. 93 Adam Berry/Getty Images; p. 97 TSgt Brian Kimball/DVIDS.

Printed in the United States of America

CONTENTS

Throughout the Cold War, both the United States and the Soviet Union sought dominance through the development and construction of deadly nuclear weapons.

The Atomic Starting Line

Beginning in elementary school, children learn about the Revolutionary War, Civil War, World War I, World War II, and other major conflicts, most of which involved disagreements over territory. As they progress into middle and high school, students memorize battles and the names of key players. Images of tanks and shotguns are stamped into their minds. However, there is one international conflict, lasting over four decades, that is often overlooked in discussions of American and world history. The Cold War, waged through tension, distance, and fear, is one of the most unique and interesting conflicts of our modern times. The events that occurred during this period have much to teach us about people, power, and **diplomacy**, the skill of managing international relations. To think that a conflict so far-reaching, long-term, and world-changing as the Cold War could be overlooked or even ignored in history classes and textbooks is a disturbing thought, as we have much to learn from what happened—and didn't happen—during the Cold War period.

This war, waged primarily between the United States and the Union of Socialist Soviet Republics (USSR), was battled on many fronts and involved numerous governments and ideologies. The two main players, who were allies against Germany during World War II, quickly built up tensions after WWII that lasted and escalated over many decades. This war included no direct, face-to-face battle between the United States and Soviet Union. Proxy wars, waged across the globe in an effort to squash or prop up the ideologies of each nation, played a major role. Korea, Vietnam, Africa, Latin America, and more were all homes to wars, some lasting years, that served the goals of the two main warring parties. Weapons, money, policies, trade deals, and even governments were swapped back and forth across the earth. This was a war of influence—each party wished to shape the map, both ideologically and physically, in order to take and keep a stronghold on the minds and hearts of everyday people. All told, more than twenty million people were killed in wars between 1945 and 1990; each one was a casualty of the ideological, economic, and power-hungry battle being waged between the superpowers, though many victims were citizens of other countries across Asia, Europe, Latin America, and Africa.

Historically, the United States has been the prime example of democracy and **capitalism,** an economic model based on private ownership and trade, and has long held up the idea of "freedom" as a standard to which other countries should strive. During World War II and the Cold War, the United States sought to contain—and later, defeat—**Communism,** a very different ideological idea that is often considered to be in opposition to democratic practice. Communism is an economic model based on communal ownership; in the USSR, this meant that most industries were controlled by the state. Over four decades, the earth appeared as a chess board in the middle of game play, with dividing lines between countries, and even within cities themselves, constantly pushing in one direction or another. Alliances were made, lands were acquired for one side or the other, and tens of billions of dollars were given over to the fight for dominance between two opposing ideas. During this time period, the lineup of key players changed many times over, and the tactics of war changed right along with them. Presidents Roosevelt, Eisenhower, Truman, Kennedy, and Reagan each fought their own versions of the war and had their own complicated relationships with Joseph Stalin, Nikita Khrushchev, Mikhail Gorbachev, and global leaders such as Chairman Mao Zedung of China, Fidel Castro of Cuba, and others.

In the following pages, we will dive deeper into what is commonly referred to as the **arms race**, the competitive acquisition and construction of more and more dangerous weapons, often used as a threat against another country. History classes are dense with discussions of the spears, shotguns, and other rudimentary weapons used in wars long past. This war, however, born out of the ashes of World War II, built itself on the threat of nuclear destruction, which enveloped the entire world. The increase, or **proliferation,** of nuclear weapons was of chief concern during the Cold War, as both the Soviet Union and the United States sought to achieve dominance through the buildup of these weapons, all while protecting the safety of their own citizens and keeping a cautious hold on the possibility of total global destruction.

Perhaps one reason why the Cold War is not often studied at length in the typical high school classroom is because the events of those fateful decades have been interpreted in a multitude of ways, and the situations that occurred were highly political and ideological, which do not make them easy to discuss. Contemporary political debates were both shaped by the Cold War and helped to shape the war itself, and these debates did not end in 1991, the final year of the war. The post–Cold War world is not one of peace. Conflicting political, social, and economic narratives still fill our daily conversations on a global scale, and the chess pieces of land disputes are ever-moving. The military-industrial complex, which emerged in the United States after World War II and blossomed during the Cold War, has not only changed the interplay of the defense industry, military, and Congress in America, but has spawned similar systems in other countries. Our economy, our political ecosystem, and our military **arsenal** have all evolved through the context of the Cold War; without these years of tensions, the daily experience of the United States citizen would have a very different look and feel.

The structures, processes, and individuals who influenced the Cold War will be discussed at length here, and we will focus on the arms race, the role played by nuclear weapons during the war, and the military-industrial complex, which has continued to grow and expand in the United States despite President Dwight D. Eisenhower's warnings against it. The trends that emerged during this time have shaped not only US foreign policy, economic policy, and military strategy in the years since, but they have also had a global effect and will continue to shape international relationships, be they peaceful or tense, in the years and decades to come.

The unofficial service emblem (circa 1946) of the Manhattan Project, a research and development operation that produced the world's first nuclear weapons

CHAPTER ONE

Mounting Tensions

A name is an extremely powerful tool. Giving a name to an item, a group, or an event can add legitimacy and even unveil or create new meaning. The man who put a formal name to the ongoing conflicts between the Soviet Union and the United States likely had no idea that he was putting forth a moniker that would thrive for the next seven decades and become a part of the global lexicon. On April 16, 1947, Bernard Baruch coined the term "Cold War" for the relations between the Soviet Union and the United States during a speech he gave at the unveiling of his own portrait. Speaking before the South Carolina legislature, the financier and advisor to Harry Truman said, "Let us not be deceived—we are today in the midst of a cold war. Our enemies are to be found abroad and at home. Let us never forget this: our unrest is the heart of their success. The peace of the world is the hope and the goal of our political system; it is the despair and defeat of those who stand against us. We can depend only on ourselves." The phrase was instantly picked up by the press to describe the bloodless, yet tense, battle being fought between the two countries. While Baruch would not live to see the end of the Cold War, his words would survive into the next century and beyond.

Most historians agree that the origins of the Cold War lie somewhere between the end of World War II in 1945 and the year of Baruch's speech, 1947. We can, however, trace the first inklings of the **arms race** and nuclear proliferation back even further, to the beginning of World War II in 1939. An arms race, as we know it today, is a competition to develop and accumulate weapons. Before the invention of nuclear weapons, countries built up arsenals, or collections of guns, tanks, naval boats, planes, and other conventional weapons. Since the beginning of time, groups of humans have desired buildups of weapons in order to appear or feel more dominant before other groups. The phrase "nuclear proliferation," on the other hand, refers to the possession of *nuclear* weapons, technology, and information, especially by countries that are not considered "nuclear weapons states" by the Nuclear Non-Proliferation Treaty, which was written in 1968. Most weapons and wars that are studied in school do not feature any type of nuclear weapons or threat whatsoever.

The Birth of the Bomb

The course of history took a radical turn, however, in October 1939, when Albert Einstein, the German-born theoretical physicist, wrote a personal letter to President Franklin Delano Roosevelt, suggesting that it is possible to use atomic fission to create a powerful weapon. **Nuclear fission** involves the splitting of atoms into fragments, creating a very large release of energy. This energy, when manipulated, can be extremely destructive. It was Einstein's fear that, following the outbreak of World War II, German scientists would be the first to develop a weapon using fission. Einstein and his Hungarian colleague, Leo Szilard, had escaped Nazism by fleeing to America, and they were deeply troubled by the idea that Hitler was already working on the bomb. They urged the United States to join the race to harness fission into an extremely powerful weapon. For four long years, American scientists worked to develop this technology.

During that time, World War II was being fought on several different fronts around the globe. The United States did not directly enter the war until 1941. At the end of that year, nuclear research intensified in America, and the **Manhattan Project** was born. This secret scientific and military undertaking was the introductory leg of what would be called the arms race. The work eventually employed more than two hundred thousand workers, including scientists, engineers, and others.

As the United States tinkered with the beginnings of a destructive weapon, the war raged on across Europe and Asia. In early 1945, three heads of government—President Franklin D. Roosevelt from the United States, Prime Minister Winston Churchill from the United Kingdom, and Premier Joseph Stalin from the Soviet Union met at what would be known as the Yalta Conference in order to discuss the reorganization of Europe after World War II. This was the second of three conferences the Big Three would convene to make a plan for post-war Europe, and it is often considered a turning point in the early years of the Cold War. The three came to the conference with assurance that the war was waning in Europe, but they were unsure of its end in the Pacific theater. Both Churchill and Roosevelt recognized that the Soviet Union could offer the key to ending the war in the Pacific. In exchange for the Soviet Union entering the war, they agreed to grant the Soviets a sphere of influence in Manchuria following Japan's surrender. The Soviets also agreed to join the United Nations, and the leaders discussed the future of Germany and Eastern Europe, each agreeing to occupy separate zones within Germany. Additionally, the Declaration of Liberated Europe, written and signed by all three leaders, promised that the people of Europe would be free to "create democratic institutions of their own choice." Later on, the breaking of this declaration would lead to an acceleration of concern and conflict during

The Big Three, Churchill, Roosevelt, and Stalin, meet at the Yalta Conference to discuss Europe's post-war reorganization.

Albert Einstein

A few months after the use of atomic bombs in Japan, *Time* magazine published an issue with an image of Einstein on its cover, backed by a ballooning mushroom cloud and the equation $E = mc^2$. The magazine article referred to Einstein as the "father of the bomb," due to his letter to the United States government that started the atomic bomb research, as well as his equation, the theory of relativity, which made the bomb theoretically possible. *Newsweek* also did a cover on Einstein, who was deeply disturbed by the attention and connection to the bomb, saying in the *Newsweek* article, "Had I known that the Germans would not succeed in producing an atomic bomb, I never would have lifted a finger."

Throughout his life, Einstein insisted that his only involvement with the atomic bomb was his letter to President Roosevelt and that he firmly identified as a pacifist. In a short essay published in 1952, Einstein wrote, "To kill in war time, it seems to me, is in no ways better than common murder."

Throughout the Cold War, Einstein would continue to be outspoken about his feelings, insisting that scientists had both the freedom to pursue knowledge and the responsibility to think about the consequences of their research. In his ideal world, scientists would make sure that the public is fully informed of their research as well as the potential risks and benefits that accompany discoveries.

the Cold War. In April, President Roosevelt would pass away from a stroke. His death was met with shock around the world, as his declining health had not been made public. He was succeeded by his vice president, Harry S. Truman.

Dropping the First Nuclear Bomb

Four months after the Yalta Conference, in July 1945, the engineers and scientists who had been working on the nuclear bomb decided that it was finally ready to test. The plutonium bomb traveled to a remote, unpopulated location in southern New Mexico. Three observation bunkers were constructed at a great distance from the test site, as no one was quite sure how much energy would be released by the bomb, or how many people would need to be evacuated due to radioactivity. The team hoped that the radioactivity would be released into the atmosphere; before this moment, however, no one in the world had ever exploded a nuclear device. This test would change the course of human history.

Just after Germany had surrendered, and while the war in the Pacific continued to rage, the first nuclear bomb was set to explode in the middle of the New Mexican desert. At five thirty in the morning on July 16, 1945, a rolling fireball exploded, completely vaporizing its tower and enveloping the surrounding area in intense heat. It stretched, spread, and developed into a mushroom shape, a vision that would become synonymous with the nuclear age, inspiring awe and fear in its wake. The successful explosion initially caused joy for those who were present, as the project they had long worked on was finally complete, and an end to the war was in sight. However, as the gravity of the success began to sink in, the staff of the Manhattan Project realized they might be forever haunted by their creation, one that would undoubtedly destroy hundreds of thousands of lives.

Ten days after the test, the United States, United Kingdom, and China all called on Japan to surrender unconditionally or face "prompt and utter destruction." The Japanese chose to ignore this threat, and on August 6, 1945, the United States dropped a uranium atomic bomb, nicknamed "Little Boy," on the city of Hiroshima, Japan. The bomb took 44.4 seconds to fall, detonating above the Shima

A cloud of smoke rises from the Japanese city of Hiroshima hours after an American B-29 bomber dropped the world's first deployed atomic bomb.

Surgical Clinic. The radius of complete destruction was about one mile while fires raged over 4.4 miles (7.1 kilometers). Seventy to eighty thousand people, or about 30% of the population of Hiroshima, were killed by the blast. About sixteen hours after the drop, President Truman called on Japan again to surrender, saying, "We may be grateful to Providence" that the German atomic bomb project had failed and that the United States and its allies had "spent two billion dollars on the greatest scientific gamble in history—and won." Truman's words at this time project a feeling of triumph, as though the arms race had been won and had thus ended. This would not prove to be the case in the coming months and years. The creation and use of the first atomic bomb had, in fact, set off the start of the arms race and the nuclear obsession that would threaten the security of the world for decades to come.

Hearing no surrender from Japan, the United States headed out just two days after the initial bombing to make a second attack. This time, the attack was on the city of Nagasaki. A large seaport town and home to many industries, Nagasaki was bombed at 11:01 in the morning on August 9. This time, a plutonium weapon was dropped, nicknamed "Fat Man." The number of estimated deaths varies wildly, numbering between twenty thousand and eighty thousand killed both at the time of the explosion and in the hours and days afterwards. As most of the buildings in Nagasaki were made of wood, the blast radius, about one mile (1.6 km), resulted in a city that was almost entirely leveled. In the months after the two bombs, many more deaths occurred due to radiation sickness, burns, and other injuries resulting from the attacks. The majority of the victims were civilians.

On August 14, 1945, the Japanese surrendered, with the emperor explaining, “I cannot endure the thought of letting my people suffer any longer.” World War II had finally ended on all fronts. The United States occupied Japan and offered the Soviet Union very little influence there, angering Stalin and adding to the post-war tension that had already begun to bubble between the United States and the USSR. Following the surrender, many people called for a ban on nuclear weapons to avoid an arms race, and Stalin

This aerial photo shows the devastated city of Nagasaki after a nuclear bomb was dropped on August 9, 1945.

assumed that the United States would return to pre-war levels of militarization and military-industrial production. However, Truman decided to keep the economy afloat through the support of military industries and continued arms creation. The capitalist slump predicted by Stalin never came to fruition.

The Soviet Union Heats Up

The Soviet Union, keen on developing their own fission bomb, began to use **espionage** tactics—spies—to retrieve blueprints for the United States' nuclear bombs. In October 1945, the head of the Soviet secret police, Lavrenty Beria, was given top-secret details of the United States' plutonium bomb by a spy working inside Los Alamos, the nuclear test facility in New Mexico. In November, the USSR signed a secret agreement with Czechoslovakia, granting them the rights to all Czechoslovakian-mined uranium, further giving the United States reason to believe that the Soviet Union was working to produce its own nuclear weapons. Finally, on Christmas Eve 1945, the United States embassy in Moscow issued a formal warning of the effort by the Soviet Union to build an atomic bomb. It was then that the nuclear arms "race" truly began in earnest.

While the discovery of Soviet nuclear efforts was a disturbing post-war realization, three other events in early 1946 marked a clear change in the attitudes of the United States and the USSR and the beginnings of what would be called the Cold War. On February 9, Joseph Stalin gave a speech at the Bolshoi Theater in Moscow that made a huge impression in the West, giving American leaders a new sense of Stalin's feelings toward the United States. In a speech on national radio, his first major public speech since the end of World War II, Stalin attacked capitalism, an economic model based on private ownership and trade, through a Communist lens. Communism is an economic model based on communal ownership; in the USSR this meant that most industries were controlled by the state. In his speech, Stalin praised the Soviet regime, blaming the war on "monopoly capitalism," and warned that future wars were inevitable due to the "present capitalist development of [the] world economy." He laid out a plan for fifteen years of military research and declared his intention to insure the Soviet Union "against any eventuality."

Stalin's speech immediately produced turmoil in Washington, DC, and London. American and British leaders were alarmed by the speech and considered it to be a threat to the West. During and just prior to his speech, Stalin had begun to put pressure on Turkey and Iran, expanding the Soviet sphere of influence and working to **annex** portions of these countries, which involved invading and occupying the territory. In the West, these movements were met with concern and distrust, and Stalin's speech only added to the turmoil, acting as a "fuse" that ignited a major change in the tone about the USSR. United States leaders suddenly realized that Stalin's expansionist goals were not going to go quietly away into the night. He was bent on unlimited Communist expansion. This caused the Truman administration to build an even deeper distrust of Stalin and to create the policy of **containment** that would define a major piece of the Cold War.

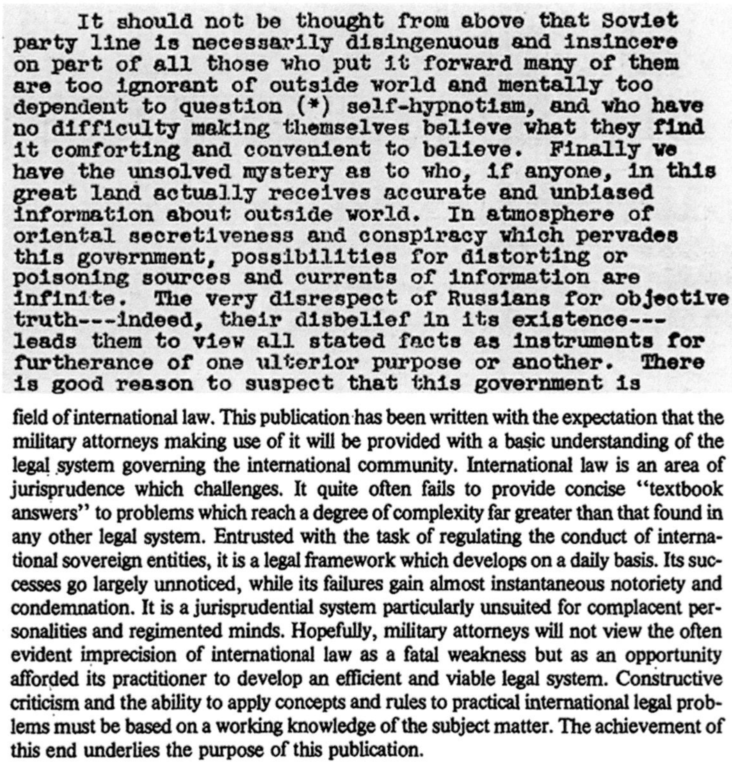

It should not be thought from above that Soviet party line is necessarily disingenuous and insincere on part of all those who put it forward many of them are too ignorant of outside world and mentally too dependent to question (*) self-hypnotism, and who have no difficulty making themselves believe what they find it comforting and convenient to believe. Finally we have the unsolved mystery as to who, if anyone, in this great land actually receives accurate and unbiased information about outside world. In atmosphere of oriental secretiveness and conspiracy which pervades this government, possibilities for distorting or poisoning sources and currents of information are infinite. The very disrespect of Russians for objective truth---indeed, their disbelief in its existence---leads them to view all stated facts as instruments for furtherance of one ulterior purpose or another. There is good reason to suspect that this government is

field of international law. This publication has been written with the expectation that the military attorneys making use of it will be provided with a basic understanding of the legal system governing the international community. International law is an area of jurisprudence which challenges. It quite often fails to provide concise "textbook answers" to problems which reach a degree of complexity far greater than that found in any other legal system. Entrusted with the task of regulating the conduct of international sovereign entities, it is a legal framework which develops on a daily basis. Its successes go largely unnoticed, while its failures gain almost instantaneous notoriety and condemnation. It is a jurisprudential system particularly unsuited for complacent personalities and regimented minds. Hopefully, military attorneys will not view the often evident imprecision of international law as a fatal weakness but as an opportunity afforded its practitioner to develop an efficient and viable legal system. Constructive criticism and the ability to apply concepts and rules to practical international legal problems must be based on a working knowledge of the subject matter. The achievement of this end underlies the purpose of this publication.

A portion of the "long telegram" sent from George Kennan to Secretary of State James Byrnes in 1946

One of the most influential underpinnings of the containment policy came from the "long telegram," an eight-thousand-word telegram sent in late February by George Kennan at the American embassy in Moscow. In response to requests for an analysis of Soviet policy, Kennan sent a telegram to the Department of State in which he spoke to the Marxist ideology and Russian imperialism that he believed motivated the country, asserting that there was an "instinctive Russian sense of insecurity" that would cause the Soviets to be deeply suspicious of other nations and seek to destroy rival powers. He pointed to the ongoing expansions in Iran and Turkey as troubling examples of expansionist tactics that would likely continue unless the West stepped up to defend the world against continued Soviet influence. Kennan also noted that the Soviet Union was "highly sensitive to logic of force" and suggested that it would back down "when strong resistance is encountered at any point." He posited that the United States and its allies would need to offer that resistance. President Truman and his circle took the telegram very seriously, using it to form foreign policy strategies for the coming years that centered on aggressively containing Soviet threat and expansion.

Following the "long telegram," Western leaders began to take a hard look at the realities of Soviet relations with the West. In March of 1946, former British Prime Minister Winston Churchill was invited to give a speech at Westminster College in Missouri. In one of the most famous speeches given during this time period, Churchill spoke of the **iron curtain** that had descended across Europe due to Soviet expansion and aggression. The Soviets saw this speech as a direct threat and invitation to begin a war between the West and the USSR. President Truman joined Churchill on the speaking platform, listening intently to Churchill's praise of the United States and call for an Anglo-American alliance against the Soviets.

The mounting tensions evident during and directly following World War II set the baseline for the long-lasting Cold War that would follow. While countries had always made efforts to out-arm others during times of war, the rise of nuclear weapons in the 1940s gave birth to the nuclear age

Going Public

The Manhattan Project, begun in 1939 as a secret United States initiative, had its "cover" blown in 1945, with the dropping of atomic bombs on Hiroshima and Nagasaki. Suddenly, the American public and the world at large were aware of what was being developed behind closed doors. The United States government had known since the beginning of the efforts that this moment would eventually come and had started public relations planning in 1944.

William Laurence, a well-known science reporter from the *New York Times* was contracted to visit atomic facilities, conduct interviews with participants, and bear witness to atomic tests, as well as the bombings. He drafted the majority of the press releases on the events.

Directly following the bombing of Hiroshima, President Harry S. Truman was the first to release a statement. Sixteen hours after the bomb dropped, Truman announced, "It is an atomic bomb." He also described the "battle of the laboratories" that ended with a weapon made by the United States and declared that America had won the battle. This was followed, after the Nagasaki bombing, with a carefully prepared report on the development of the atomic bomb.

The public relations efforts proved, initially, to be successful—a 1945 poll showed that eighty-five percent of respondents approved of the use of the atomic bomb. However, public opinion would eventually become more varied, as newspapers, magazines, and airways began to fill with other opinions about the future of nuclear energy, foreign policy, and defense efforts.

and an "arms race" that would soon envelop both the United States and the USSR in military research efforts, increased military spending, and the development of more accurate, far-reaching, and destructive weapons. As we will see, in coming decades, the race for armament would be aided by the forming of the military-industrial complex, an alliance between the military and the defense industry that would use the private sector to produce sophisticated weapons in extreme numbers. While the world powers thought they were resolving tensions from World War II and creating a foundation of peaceful relations, the first sparks of the Cold War were stoked and stirred.

President Truman, surrounded by members of Congress, signs the NATO (North Atlantic Treaty Organization) pact, hoping to contain possible Soviet aggression against Western Europe.

CHAPTER TWO

Nuclear Proliferation, the Military-Industrial Complex, and the Arms Race

When Bernard Baruch coined the phrase "Cold War" to describe the ongoing tensions between the United States and the Soviet Union, he touched on two truths: first, the two nations were engaged in a war, an armed conflict. Second, the war was not a "hot" situation with active shooting and bombs exchanged between the two countries, but a "cold" one, built on threats in statements and speeches, aggressive policy decisions, and a consistent arms buildup. The war being waged between these two countries, however, was not fought in isolation. The Cold War was felt around the world—in proxy wars in other nations, through strategic spending on military research and manufacturing, and through the fear, felt by those across the globe, that the world could be destroyed through the unfettered use of nuclear weapons. Citizens of all nations became spectators of the arms "race" engaged in by

Political cartoons, like this one depicting President Eisenhower and Prime Minister Churchill shouting to Soviet leader Nikolai Bulganin atop piles of nuclear bombs, were a popular form of commentary during the Cold War years.

the Soviet Union and the United States, and some countries were even thrown into the competition—housing weapons, making weapons, or helping to finance the manufacturing and research efforts.

Cold War Alliances

NATO

One of the first events that pushed the arms race between two countries into a competition with global involvement was the movement of the United States into the North Atlantic Treaty Organization (**NATO**). NATO was the first mutual security and military alliance in which the United States had chosen to engage. Signed on April 4, 1949, the NATO agreement stated that, in the event of an attack by an external party, any member country would jump to the defense of any other member country. The precursor to NATO, the Treaty of Brussels, was signed in 1948, and included member states Belgium, the Netherlands, Luxembourg, France, and the United Kingdom. Soon after, it was decided that the United States should be included in the alliance in order to offer a true defense against the Soviet Union. The new association included the five countries from the Treaty of Brussels, as well as Canada, Denmark, Iceland, Italy, Norway, Portugal, and the United States. The NATO treaty not only cemented the member countries as each other's defenders; it began a trajectory of military exercises, arms buildup as called for by the NATO Military Committee, and human force buildup of incredible size. NATO forces were put in place in strategic locations to ensure a quick and strong defense should any of the member countries face attack. NATO also brought about a standardization of military technologies—member nations, beginning in the early 1950s, adopted standard weapons and other technology, which necessitated, as we'll see in detail later, a major ramp-up in weapons manufacturing.

The Warsaw Pact

In response to NATO, the Soviet Union and seven of its European satellites signed their own alliance treaty. This document, called the Warsaw Pact, wasn't drawn up until

1955, spurred by the entering of West Germany into NATO. The Warsaw Pact countries saw the inclusion of West Germany into NATO and the decision to remilitarize the zone as a direct threat. The treaty, signed in Warsaw just two weeks after the inclusion of West Germany, included Albania, Bulgaria, Czechoslovakia, East Germany, Hungary, Poland, Romania, and the Soviet Union. Like NATO, the Warsaw Pact was a military alliance, creating defense ties between each of the countries involved. It also allowed the Soviet Union to have even tighter control over European satellites. The wait between NATO and the Warsaw Pact signings are one example of the ways in which the Cold War did not fit a strict "action-reaction" model. When one country made a move, the other did not immediately respond with equal or greater force. The lack of linear, predictable moves throughout the duration of the conflict made the Cold War a war of unknowns, which only added to the ever-present tension.

The Arms Race

After the release of the first atomic bombs on Nagasaki and Hiroshima, the United States did not put an end to weapons manufacturing. In fact, President Truman, acting in accordance with the threats he perceived from the Soviet Union, decided to strategically build up the United States's arsenal of weapons, including nuclear warheads. By 1947, the cache was still relatively small, with between twenty and fifty weapons. At that time, the American Joint Chiefs of Staff had declared that one hundred fifty weapons would be enough to completely defend the United States from a Soviet threat. The manufacture of weapons was key for the NATO nations and the United States, as the Soviet Union was plowing ahead, successfully, with its efforts to create an atomic bomb. The United States government theorized that the Soviets were years away from such a weapon, dating its possible explosion to the mid-1950s. However, the world was shocked when, on August 29, 1949, merely four years after the attacks on Hiroshima and Nagasaki, the Soviet Union successfully tested its first atomic bomb, code-named "RDS-1," in modern-day Kazakhstan. The RDS-1 bore a very close resemblance to "Fat Man," the plutonium bomb dropped on Nagasaki. The United States, quickly realizing that its nuclear monopoly had been broken, almost immediately amped up the production of atomic fission weapons, while also pushing ahead with their research of nuclear fusion (also called "hydrogen") weapons. A hydrogen bomb had the potential to be exponentially more destructive than fission bombs, and many scientists were opposed to its creation, but Truman held the strong belief that a more advanced weapon would keep the United States ahead in the newly active and competitive arms race.

The H-Bomb

During this same year, the Soviets gained a major advance with the triumph of Communism in China. The nationalists were defeated in the Chinese Civil War, creating a "Sino-Soviet bloc" that stretched from Europe to Asia. With the addition of the war in Korea heating up in 1950, President Truman decided to begin tests on what would be called the

When detonated, a hydrogen bomb creates a "mushroom cloud," a distinctly shaped cloud of debris, smoke, and condensed water vapor.

"H-bomb," or hydrogen bomb. On November 1, 1952, three days before the 1952 general election, the United States conducted a test, code-named "Mike," detonating a hydrogen device in the Pacific. The detonation vaporized an entire island and left a crater more than a mile wide. Little more than a year had passed since the first formal super bomb research had begun. The destruction caused by the bomb was incredible and terrifying. The boundless power of the H-bomb was clear not only to successful scientists in the United States but also to countries around the world who were watching, waiting, and working on weapons programs of their own.

In the 1952 election, Dwight D. Eisenhower was elected president, opening up the opportunity for a new path when it came to nuclear weapons and the ongoing arms race. Eisenhower entered office with new goals and ideas about how the United States would function militarily across the globe. While Truman had built up conventional forces used to fight the Korean War, Eisenhower desired to rely less on conventional manpower and weapons, instead hoping to capitalize on the growing nuclear arsenal. The Soviet Union had caught up quickly, testing a hybrid bomb in 1953 and detonating their own "true" H-bomb in 1955. Throughout the Cold War, the United States would conduct 1,032 official nuclear tests; the Soviet Union would conduct 715.

Deterrence

During the early 1950s, both the United States and NATO together developed the idea of **deterrence.** This concept was an attempt to forestall enemy attacks by making a credible threat of retaliation. For example, if the United States kept up its nuclear arsenal and was about to massively retaliate in the event of any attack, the Soviet Union and other countries would not choose to attack, thereby avoiding all-out war and mutually assured destruction. With an American threat to initiate nuclear war, there would be no Communist offensive

Dwight D. Eisenhower served as United States president from 1953 to 1961 and has long been considered one of the greatest United States presidents.

against the European democracies. The leaders of the Soviet Union, on the other hand, believed that a nuclear war could be fought—and won.

During the Eisenhower years in the 1950s, the arms race picked up to a quick pace. By this time, large-scale atomic bombs were not the only weapons sitting in the two countries' respective arsenals. Defensive weapons, including missiles, bombers, spy planes, and more were stockpiled in the United States and Soviet Union in order to prepare for an attack from the other side of the ocean. Wernher von Braun, one of the most controversial figures during this time period, was a key player in the creation of nuclear ballistic missiles for the United States. In the USSR, early missile development centered on missiles capable of attacking European targets. Their first successful nuclear missile test occurred in 1957. These weapons were called **intercontinental ballistic missiles** (ICBM). These rockets were capable of traveling thousands of miles to strategically deliver nuclear weapons to specific targets. During this time period, then-leader of the Soviets, Nikita Khrushchev, claimed that the Soviet Union had total dominance in the field of ICBM production, which would leave the United States too weak to deal with Soviet threats. Eisenhower did his best to counter these claims by using spy planes, such as the U-2 plane, to keep a close eye on Soviet weapons development. In 1960, a Russian missile shot down a U-2 plane and captured its pilot, who admitted to American spying. This incident was a huge embarrassment for Eisenhower and the United States. It also overshadowed the fact that the Americans had actually started to pull ahead in the arms race, producing missiles at ever-advancing rates.

Around 1960, talk of militarizing began to dominate the presidential election. Eager to see how a new president would change, again, the course of the Cold War, American citizens readied themselves to move from Truman-era and Eisenhower-era military policies to a third take on the ever-tense relations between the United States and the Soviet Union. A young democrat, John F. Kennedy, promised to enlarge American nuclear forces once again and criticized Eisenhower for allowing Cuba to turn Communist, among other perceived missteps. Kennedy assured voters that he would protect American nuclear dominance and increase military production on an even larger scale. During this period, France conducted its own tests, becoming the third nuclear power in the world. Though unlikely to strike either the United States or the Soviet Union independently, France's coming into the nuclear age represented, for many, a change in the global atomic narrative—nuclear weapons were no longer a privilege of the two superpowers, but a necessity for safety in an ever-militarized global world.

The Military-Industrial Complex

As he readied himself to leave office, President Eisenhower observed the proliferation of nuclear weapons, the arms race, and the increasing militarization of the world around him. In his farewell speech on January 17, 1961, Eisenhower introduced us to a new phrase: the military-industrial complex. As a fiscal conservative and Republican, Eisenhower was concerned about the rising costs of weapons production, which included not only conventional weapons for United States military branches, but also the export of weapons to

NATO countries and nations involved in proxy wars, as well as submarines, bomber planes, spy planes, vehicles, and, of course, nuclear warheads. In the United States, there would emerge a very close relationship between the military and the defense industry which supplies it. The United States, in the coming decades, would spend more on its military each year than any other nation. This spending trend continues today.

In 1961, as President Kennedy took office, he met with Khrushchev for a first conversation and negotiation. The Soviet leader, judging Kennedy to be weak and likely to succumb to pressure, bullied the new president. Kennedy

President Eisenhower gives his farewell speech from the Oval Office, warning listeners about the possibility of the military-industrial complex.

decided to take a hard line with his policies regarding the ongoing war, ordering a new national fallout shelter program in order to provide defense in the event of a nuclear attack. By this time, both the United States and the Soviet Union had built up impressive arsenals, but the United States was still ahead in the "missile gap" between the two. Following the Soviet placement of missiles in Cuba, ninety miles (144.8 km) from the American mainland, and the crisis that followed, the United States took time to reexamine its nuclear policies once more. In 1962, the United States, now sure of its superior second-strike capabilities due to stockpiles of new ICBMs and submarine-launched ballistic missiles, adopted a new doctrine: assured destruction. In this scenario, the United States could reasonably assume the ability to destroy the Soviet Union even after a Soviet first strike. However, if the conditions were such that both sides had second-strike capabilities, the situation would be described as **mutually assured destruction**, or MAD. This concept provided ample reason for caution at times of crisis, as both sides could assure the destruction of the other.

Treaties: Signs of Progress

During the years of MAD, both NATO countries and the Soviet bloc continued to increase their nuclear arsenals and perform nuclear tests. Public anxiety over nuclear testing began to rise as more information became available surrounding the nuclear fallout that occurred during testing of weapons, particularly H-bombs. In an effort to prevent even more radioactive material from entering the earth's atmosphere and causing health problems, and at least partially in an attempt to slow nuclear proliferation, the Partial Nuclear Test Ban Treaty was signed in Moscow on August 5, 1963, by the United States, the United Kingdom, and the Soviet Union. This treaty, the very first major nuclear arms control agreement, prohibited nuclear explosions in the atmosphere, in outer space, and underwater. The ban did create a decline in the presence of radioactive particles in the atmosphere, but it did not slow nuclear proliferation. In 1964, China became the fifth nuclear power, following the United States, Soviet Union, United Kingdom, and France.

In order to combat nuclear proliferation, Soviet leader Leonid Brezhnev and United States president Lyndon B. Johnson worked together to write the Treaty on the Non-Proliferation of Nuclear Weapons (NPNW). Signed on July 1, 1968, the treaty is still the world's most widely accepted arms control agreement. The treaty came into force in 1970, as signatories agreed that companies outside of the five that already held weapons would not test nuclear weapons. Nuclear material could only be used for electric power. Additionally, the United States, Britain, France, the Soviet Union, and China all agreed not to assist other nations with the development of nuclear weapons. By the 2000s, one hundred eighty-nine nations had signed on. In order to make sure countries are in accordance with the treaty, the Atomic Energy Agency, an arm of the United Nations, completes inspections of nuclear facilities in all signing nations. As of 2003, all members of the United Nations, except Israel, India, and Pakistan, had signed the Nuclear Non-Proliferation Treaty, while one member, North Korea, has recently threatened to withdraw. Much more

The United Nations headquarters, located in New York City, is surrounded by 193 flags: one for each member nation and one United Nations flag.

than the Partial Nuclear Test Ban Treaty, the NPNW did much to assure that nuclear weapons would not continue to proliferate outside of their current bounds. However, this does not mean that nuclear arsenals would not continue to build up within the nuclear-holding countries.

The research and production of missiles and weapons continued throughout the 1960s and 1970s in both the United States and Soviet Union. It wasn't until the early 1970s that productive talks began and treaties were written in order to attempt to slow down arms buildups and truly put an end to nuclear proliferation. In 1967, President Johnson was the first to suggest talks on the limitation of arms production. The next year, the Soviet Union agreed, and the two began full-scale negotiations in November 1969. These negotiations were specifically aimed at curtailing the manufacture of strategic missiles capable of carrying nuclear weapons. The first agreement, known as SALT I, or the Strategic Arms Limitation Treaty, was signed in 1972 by the United States and the Soviet Union. The treaty limited the growth of strategic arsenals. At the summit meeting in Moscow, President Richard M. Nixon and Brezhnev agreed to a complex set of agreements, the two key components being the Treaty on Anti-Ballistic Missile (ABM) Systems and the Interim Agreement and Protocol on Limitation of Strategic Offensive Weapons.

Anti-ballistic missiles, or ABMs, were created to counter ICBMs, or missiles carrying nuclear warheads launched by the other superpower. These surface-to-air missiles were designed to intercept and destroy ballistic threats. The ABM Treaty limited the United States and the Soviet Union to one ABM deployment area per superpower and only one hundred interceptor missiles at each missile-launching site. The Interim Agreement froze the number of ICBMs and SLBMs (submarine-launched ballistic missiles) at current levels for five years. These agreements, put together, were the first of their kind that truly put a cap on the production of weapons on both sides of the war. Unfortunately, SALT I didn't go quite far enough. Other types of weapons, such as bombers and other strategic launchers, were not covered under SALT I, so the Soviet Union and United

The Atlas, the first intercontinental ballistic missile developed by the United States, is deployed from a test site.

States continued to research and develop newer and better defenses. Each country focused on a different strategic force: the United States worked on development of smaller missiles with great accuracy while the Soviet Union put its time and energy into missiles with large warheads. SALT II agreements went on for seven years, finally ending with

"A Shaft of Sunlight is Breaking Through"

After four long and dark decades of the Cold War, the early 1990s signaled a break in the clouds for Americans who had lived through the years of near-constant tension between the United States and the Soviet Union. Reporting on September 29, 1991, the *Chicago Tribune* recorded President Bush's announcement of drastic arms reductions. The article read, "Declaring that recent changes in the former Soviet Union had made it possible, the president announced deep unilateral cuts in the United States nuclear arsenal, including the elimination of all short-range, land- or sea-launched nukes, and he challenged the Soviet successor states to match the [United States] in a number of other dramatic moves." The president's announcement followed the Strategic Arms Reduction Treaty he signed with Mikhail Gorbachev in July 1991, as well as the collapse of the Kremlin.

Following this informal "end" to the war, politicians on both sides of the aisle attempted to take credit for winning the war, though it is difficult to declare a true winner, as no direct confrontation ever took place. Some argue that the arms race brought the Soviet economy to an unmanageable state. Others suggest that the containment of Communism was the key to ending both the war and the Kremlin itself. We do know, at least, that 1991 ushered in a new era of conversations for both the United States and the Soviet Union—talk was no longer of nuclear weapons, missile crises, and superpower enemies. Both countries began to look toward the years ahead, life beyond the Cold War, and how to ensure security and prosperity amidst other global threats, such as terrorism.

the signing of the new treaty in 1979. The treaty, in its final form, set limits on the number of heavy bombers, multiple independently targeted reentry vehicle ICBMs and SLBMs, and strategic launchers. Each side was allowed a total number of about 2,400 of such weapons. Brezhnev and President Jimmy Carter signed the agreement in Vienna on June 18, 1979. The two superpowers continued to observe SALT II over the next few years, even as conflicts arose and cooled between them.

Negotiation

The next and even more impactful round of arms control negotiations occurred in the early 1980s and spanned three decades. These talks and the subsequent agreement, known as START I, aimed to reduce the holds of nuclear warheads, bombers, and missiles in both countries. President Ronald Reagan, taking office after almost forty years of Cold War conflict and negotiations, proposed radical reductions in each side's arsenal. This stood in stark contrast to the policies of presidents past, such as Truman, who desired a buildup of weapons, and Kennedy during the MAD years, who thought it a best case scenario if each side could assure the destruction of the other. Reagan hoped to turn the tide, pushing the conversation into one of active disarmament for both sides. The arms control talks started and stopped amidst an eventful 1980s and 1990s that saw the NATO-backed United States deployment of intermediate-range cruise missiles in Western Europe and the breakup of the Soviet Union. In 1991, START I was signed by President George H.W. Bush and Soviet leader Mikhail Gorbachev.

Atomic Playgrounds

Nuclear proliferation, the arms race, and the military-industrial complex weren't simply ideas carried out between politicians and diplomats. They were realities felt every day by those living in the United States, Soviet Union, and other countries associated with and affected by the Cold War. Books, movies, music, and television shows all reflected the culture of the Cold War. One of the most unique ways that the youngest citizens experienced the war was through the most common, everyday structure—playground equipment. Playgrounds are central to the lives of most children, as they appear near schools, in parks, throughout residential neighborhoods, and in public spaces such as downtowns and recreation centers. Playgrounds are one of the only spaces that are constructed for the sole purpose of giving children a free outlet for enjoyment and exercise. In the 1950s and 1960s, in both Communist and non-Communist countries, the trend in playground equipment took a turn from generic swings, teeter-totters, and merry-go-rounds and veered into the arms race. Suddenly, it was not uncommon to see rocket ships, missiles, submarines, and "atomic" or "radar" shapes.

Though the end of the Cold War brought with it new regulations and styles that all but wiped out the popularity of "atomic playgrounds," one can still find these vintage structures today, both in North America and across Europe. Some local governments are now grappling with the historical value of such structures in our current culture, where accessibility and safety are necessary. These governments will need to find new ways to preserve these unique, domestic markers of the Cold War while still prioritizing the ever-important mission of positive, safe play.

The agreement limited the number of warheads, missiles, and other weapons allowed in both the United States and Russia. The destruction of missiles was carried out over several years; the United States and Russia did not reach the required levels until 1997.

In the midst of the negotiations between the signing of SALT I and SALT II, India conducted successful nuclear weapon tests. India was not a signatory of the Nuclear Proliferation Treaty, and it would continue to abstain from signing. Since then, several other countries have performed nuclear tests or suggested that they would or could start their own nuclear weapons programs. Though treaties and agreements would help to cool down the conflicts of the Cold War, they would never be the end-all-be-all answer to stopping nuclear proliferation. Once the nuclear age had dawned, it would be next to impossible to put an end to the ever-growing list of countries with nuclear interests, as well as the speed with which the military-industrial complex moved along in America and other countries, pushing us all into less of an arms "race" and more of a continued day-to-day existence of being "armed and ready" for anything at all.

Edward Teller is known as the father of the hydrogen bomb.

CHAPTER THREE

The Faces of the Cold War

An "armed and ready" America, and likewise, a Soviet Union prepared for the worst, would not have been possible without the planning, decisions, and actions made by an "army" of politicians, scientists, engineers, businessmen, and military leaders. Without a great many actors, the Cold War may have resulted in true nuclear non-proliferation, or a decision to disarm altogether, or, in the worst-case scenario, a misuse of nuclear weapons that ended the world as we would come to know it. In this chapter, we will learn more about the key players in the arms race, including those who sought to speed up the production of nuclear weapons and those who hoped to prevent their existence and eventual use. Political leaders, such as President Truman and President Eisenhower, as well as Mikhail Gorbachev, were tasked with leading their countries through times of conflict and developing military policy in the midst of changing understandings of warfare and advancing technologies. Others, like Edward Teller,

Wernher von Braun, and J. Robert Oppenheimer, were the pioneering physicists and scientists who created some of the most powerful and potentially catastrophic weapons of the modern age. In order to paint a thorough and complete picture of the ins and outs of nuclear proliferation, the arms race, and Eisenhower's famed military-industrial complex, it is important to touch on the lives of each of these men; only then can we clearly see the ways in which political leadership and scientific discovery joined together during the Cold War to both fuel and temper the conflicts that occurred over the course of four ever-evolving decades.

Edward Teller

Edward Teller was born in Budapest, Hungary in 1908. At that time, neither Edward nor his loving parents or siblings knew that he would someday be known as the "father of the hydrogen bomb." It is hard to imagine staring down at your beautiful, new baby boy with the knowledge that he would one day create the world's most destructive weapons, participating in the production of the atomic bomb and later leading the development of the H-bomb. Teller, born into a prosperous Jewish family, was also born during one of the most turbulent times in Hungarian history. Following a briefly successful Communist regime following the First World War, the country was ruled by an anti-Semitic fascist dictator, Miklos Horthy, beginning in 1920. Teller was pleased to leave his homeland for Germany in 1926. There, he earned a degree in chemical engineering, eventually receiving his PhD in theoretical physics. It was during his time in

Munich that Teller was involved in a streetcar accident, which severed his foot, forcing him to wear a prosthetic foot for the remainder of his life. His struggles in Germany, however, did not end with a violently injured leg; as Hitler came to power, Teller knew it was time to leave. He would later tell his biographer, "the hope of making an academic career in Germany for a Jew existed before Hitler came and vanished the day he arrived." In 1935, Teller emigrated to the United States and acquired a teaching position at George Washington University in Washington, DC. Living within the country's political center and daily immersing himself in the science of nuclear physics encouraged Teller's drive to defend the United States against Nazism and led him to devote his energies to developing nuclear weapons. He was one of the first scientists recruited to work on the Manhattan Project, the secret program to create an atomic bomb. Though the fission A-bomb project kept Teller busy, he began to think deeply about the possibility of an even more powerful, thermonuclear hydrogen fusion bomb.

Driven by the dropping of atomic bombs at Hiroshima and Nagasaki, as well as the Soviet Union's successful test in 1949, Teller became even more determined to create the H-bomb. After the discovery of Soviet spies in American nuclear labs, President Truman sounded the all-clear for continued research on the hydrogen bomb at Los Alamos in New Mexico. After its Pacific atoll test in 1951, the H-bomb was deemed a success, and Teller was named the "the father of the H-bomb." Ever-stubborn, staunchly anti-Communist, and fiercely devoted to the security of the United States, Edward Teller continued to help develop American nuclear labs, opposed the Nuclear Test Ban Treaty, and eventually testified against Robert J. Oppenheimer, a fellow nuclear physicist, on the grounds that Oppenheimer had continually opposed the H-bomb and aligned himself with left-leaning groups. Teller's outspoken rejection of Oppenheimer, a loyal and hardworking researcher, grew into a rift between Teller himself and the wider scientific community. A tireless and true believer in nuclear defense, Teller was awarded the Presidential Medal of Freedom in 2003, just before his death at the age of 95.

Robert J. Oppenheimer

The man Edward Teller would eventually denounce amid outcry from the scientific community, Robert J. Oppenheimer, began his life not unlike Teller did, born into a Jewish family at the turn of the twentieth century. His early life was characterized by his family's involvement in the Ethical Culture Society, an outgrowth of American Reform Judaism. This organization emphasized social justice, civic responsibility, and secular humanism, and Oppenheimer, clearly gifted from a young age, was an active participant. A New Yorker who often vacationed on Long Island, he pursued higher education at Harvard University, and then in England and Germany, eventually ending up with advanced degrees in theoretical physics. He accepted professorships at the University of California, Berkeley, and the California Institute of Technology. While on the West Coast, Oppenheimer reacted to the rise of Nazism and the dawn of the Great Depression by plunging into left-wing politics. About the Depression's impact on his students'

General Leslie R. Groves and J. Robert Oppenheimer examine the Trinity site following the successful test.

abilities to obtain work, Oppenheimer said, "I began to understand how deeply political and economic events could affect men's lives." He began to involve himself and donate annually to funds associated with the Communist Party.

In 1941, Oppenheimer was brought onto the Manhattan Project, along with Edward Teller and other promising scientists. It was Oppenheimer who chose Los Alamos, the top-secret A-bomb testing facility. From 1943 to 1945, Oppenheimer served as director of the Los Alamos Laboratory. Though he is often referred to as the "father of the atomic bomb," Oppenheimer was also a family man; his second child, Katherine, was born at Los Alamos.

Following the destruction of Nagasaki and Hiroshima, Oppenheimer would resign as director of Los Alamos, taking a new position as the director of the Institute for Advanced Study in Princeton, New Jersey. He went on to become the chairman of the General Advisory Committee of the Atomic Energy Commission. In 1949, the Commission took a stand and opposed the development of the hydrogen bomb, Edward Teller's passion project. As the early 1950s were the height of anti-Communist feelings in the United States, Oppenheimer was accused of having Communist sympathies. In 1953, just thirty-two hours before it was set to expire, Oppenheimer was stripped of his security clearance. The public ordeal was devastating to his career, and, despite impassioned testimony from many of his supporters, his clearance was never reinstated. Oppenheimer returned to academic life, teaching, lecturing, and continuing to support international control of atomic energy until his death from throat cancer in 1967.

Harry S. Truman

Just as Robert J. Oppenheimer and Edward Teller, fathers of the A-bomb and H-bomb, respectively, were devoting their professional lives to the research and production of nuclear weapons, those in the White House and Congress were making decisions behind the scenes, examining the threats of Soviet attack and Communist expansion and authorizing the Manhattan Project—which would soon catapult the two physicists to success, even as the fission bomb would devastate tens of thousands of lives. Harry S. Truman, who would serve as the thirty-third president between 1945 and 1953, had little background information to inform him when he took office on April 12, 1945. He served as vice president under President Franklin D. Roosevelt, and it is reported that during that short time, Truman received no briefing on the development of the atomic bomb or the conflicts, as they unfolded, with Soviet Russia. The challenges he would face in the next eight years, including those surrounding nuclear weapons, were enormous and varied; after Roosevelt's sudden death, he took up his new job with diligence, quickly bringing himself up to speed on all of the timely issues.

Born in 1884 in Lamar, Missouri, Truman grew up just east of Kansas City, in Independence, Missouri. This city is often known as the "Queen City of the Trails" because it is the jumping-off point for the Oregon, California, and Santa Fe trails. In this gateway to the West, Truman prospered as a farmer, oil driller, and banker for twelve years. During this time, he fell in love with his wife, with

President Truman, shown here in the Oval Office, served as United States president from 1945 to 1953.

whom he would later start a family. In 1917, Truman's National Guard unit was shipped to France to fight the First World War. While there, he was promoted to captain, and after the war, he served in the reserves, eventually rising to the rank of colonel. After a failed turn as the owner of a haberdashery, Truman was elected to the role of judge on the Jackson County Court in 1922. As a judge, he gained a reputation for honesty and efficiency in management. In 1934, Truman became a United States senator, and he served in that role until 1944, when he ran for vice president with President Franklin D. Roosevelt. Just eighty-two days after the pair was sworn into office, President Roosevelt unexpectedly passed away, and Truman stepped up. In his first year in office, which he would later refer to as the "year of decisions," Truman authorized the bombing of Hiroshima and Nagasaki, prompting Japan to surrender and effectively ending World War II. He also signed the charter ratifying the United Nations, a move that he hoped would improve peaceful relations across the globe. However, Truman's authorization of the atomic bomb is still considered one of the most controversial decisions of any American president. While the president made many changes to United States foreign policy and established domestic programs intended to grow the economy at home, Truman may be best remembered for the atomic bombing, as well as his decision to enter the Korean War. After two terms of office, President Truman moved home to Independence, Missouri to live out the rest of his life until he died at the age of eighty-eight.

Dwight D. Eisenhower

Directly following Truman's presidency, United States citizens felt the need for a new and different type of commander, one who would hopefully ease tensions with Russia in the years following the start of the Cold War. With the irresistible slogan "I Like Ike," Dwight D. Eisenhower easily won victory in the presidential election of 1952. A midwesterner at heart, like Truman, President Eisenhower grew up in Abilene, Kansas. He was born in 1890 to a poor, devout Mennonite family that believed strongly in pacifism. To his mother's dismay, Eisenhower entered the US Military Academy at West Point. Following graduation, he had hoped to be deployed, but World War I ended just before he was scheduled to go. He served as a military aid to General John J. Pershing, and later to General Douglas MacArthur, eventually being promoted to captain, receiving the Distinguished Service Medal. Between World War I and World War II, Eisenhower graduated from the army's Command and General Staff School at Fort Leavenworth, Kansas. Two years later, he graduated from the Army War College. During World War II, Eisenhower was made a full general and began preparing strategy for an Allied invasion of Europe; on D-day, he was the Supreme Commander of the troops invading France. In December 1944, Eisenhower was made a five-star general. Upon his return to the states, Eisenhower worked under President Truman for two years, directing the demobilization of the wartime army. Then, after leaving active duty, Eisenhower excelled as president of Columbia University and commander

One of the most well-known and catchiest political slogans of all time, "I Like Ike," helped to draft Dwight D. Eisenhower out of private citizenship and into the presidency.

of NATO forces. In 1952, he was finally persuaded to make a run for the presidency.

In a sweeping victory, Dwight D. Eisenhower became President Eisenhower, and over the next eight years he would work to develop foreign policy that concentrated on maintaining world peace. Soon after taking office, he signed an armistice ending the Korean War. He developed an "atoms for peace" program to loan American uranium to other countries for peaceful purposes and sought to improve relations with the Soviet Union, especially following the

I Like Ike

President Dwight D. Eisenhower was the first American presidential candidate to be "drafted" by United States citizens. Eisenhower was not a career politician who always had the White House on his mind. However, he was eventually persuaded to make the move from his military career to the life of a presidential candidate for the Republican party and, eventually, to a life as president of the United States. "I Like Ike" was a campaign song featured in the very first political commercial that ever aired on television, produced by Walt Disney Studios. The feel-good commercial featured a bouncy elephant and a catchy beat, the combination of which helped him win the presidency and experience a positive, rosy beginning to his time in office.

When his time came to leave office in 1961, voters were looking toward the incoming president, John F. Kennedy, with optimism and excitement. This may explain why reactions to his farewell address were muted, with little comment given from listeners, even after Eisenhower issued his warnings about the military-industrial complex. Speaking of the armaments industry, he said, "This conjunction of an immense military establishment and a large arms industry is new in the American experience. The total influence—economic, political, even spiritual—is felt in every city, every Statehouse, every office of the Federal government." His words here, and elsewhere throughout the address, were urgent and serious. Unfortunately, history tells us that his call to care and action was not heeded on the scale that he would have hoped.

death of Joseph Stalin in 1953. While in office, Eisenhower had hopes of signing a treaty with the Soviet Union, but his vision never came to fruition. However, his approval ratings remained high throughout his tenure as president, and he gave a farewell address in 1961 that warned of the influence of the military-industrial complex, a force that could impact foreign relations through an unnatural partnership between the military and private sector. Eisenhower passed away in 1969, after many years in retirement at his farm in Gettysburg, Pennsylvania, where he authored several books.

Klaus Fuchs

While Harry Truman, Dwight Eisenhower, John F. Kennedy, and Ronald Reagan all headed up the executive branch of government during the Cold War, and American scientific geniuses crafted the nuclear weapons we are familiar with today, one could argue that no one had quite as much influence on the events of the time as the Soviets who engaged in espionage to assure Soviet dominance during the war. Emil Klaus Julius Fuchs, better known as Klaus Fuchs, was born in Germany in 1911. While studying physics and mathematics, Fuchs joined the German Communist party in 1930. When the Nazis came to power in 1933, Fuchs and his family were forced to flee Germany for France and then Great Britain, where he continued his studies and received his doctorate. At the start of World War II, Fuchs was briefly interned in Canada as a German. However, he was soon released to do research on the atomic bomb at the University of Birmingham, where he signed a pledge of secrecy. During the war, he was invited to participate in the Manhattan Project and proceeded to travel to Los Alamos, New Mexico. He was invited to help with the research due to his expertise in physics. Unfortunately, while working on the project, we now know that he continually passed on his knowledge of the theory and design of the atomic bomb to the Soviets. It was reported that Dr. Fuchs said, "When I learned the purpose of the work, I decided to inform Russia, and I established contact through another member of the Communist Party." He had no hesitation in supplying the Soviets with any and all information he had.

In 1950, after a routine security check of Fuchs's father, British authorities received word that the American FBI (Federal Bureau of Investigation) had decoded a Soviet message that indicated Fuchs was a Russian spy. He was arrested on February 3, 1950. Following his arrest, Fuchs admitted to funneling top-secret information to the Soviets since 1943. He was sentenced to fourteen years in prison, due to the fact that his espionage is said to have saved the Soviets at least one year, if not two years, in their own creation of the atomic bomb. In 1959, Fuchs was released from prison for good behavior, and he moved to East Germany to live with his father and resume his science career. He continued to commit himself to Communism, receiving many honors from the East German Communist Party. Though Fuchs continued to live in relative peace following his move to East Germany, his arrest set off a chain of events that led to the capture of several other Soviet sympathizers. David Greenglass, another employee at the Manhattan Project, and Harry Gold, who Fuchs said was the middleman between

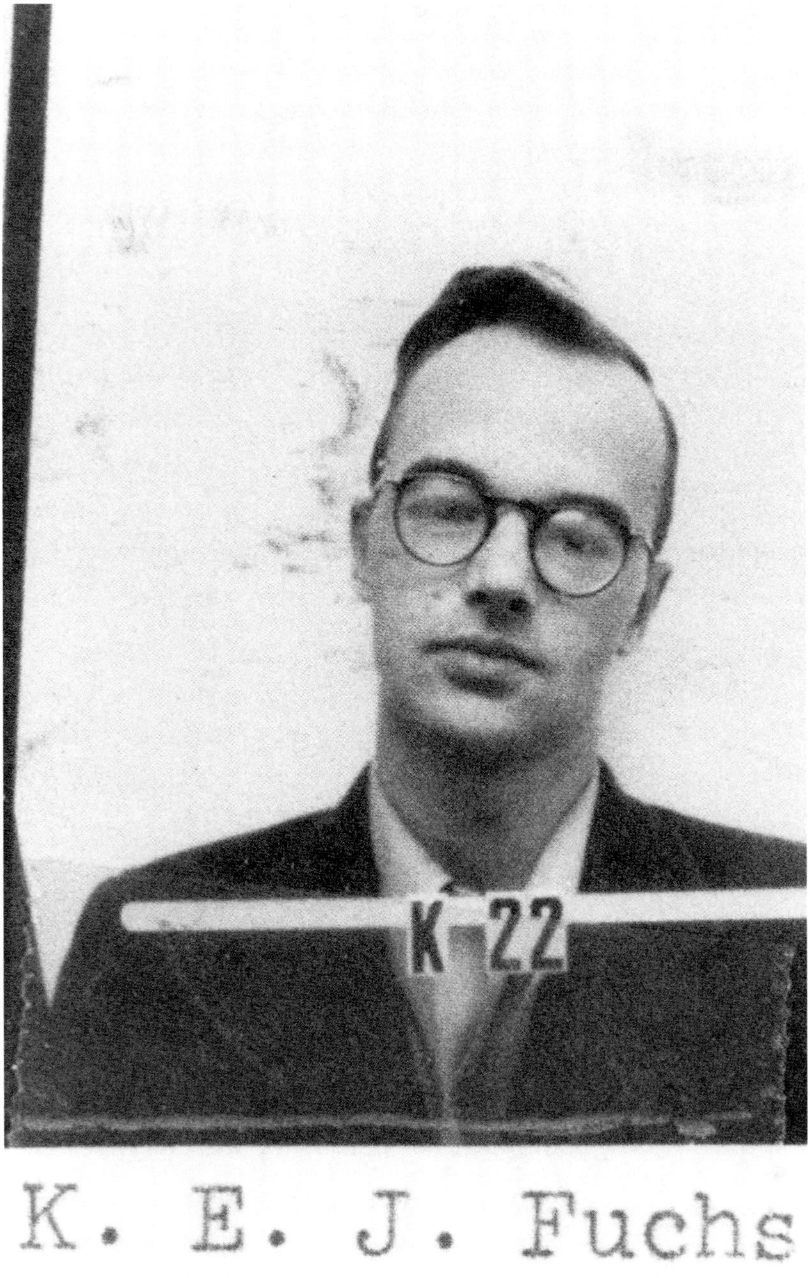

The security badge of atomic spy Klaus Fuchs allowed him access to the Los Alamos National Laboratory, where classified nuclear research and tests take place.

himself and Russia, were both captured, as well as Ethel and Julius Rosenberg, the most well-known of those convicted of espionage during the Cold War period. They were found guilty and executed in 1953.

Joseph Stalin

Cold War espionage was at once the subject of popular American books, movies, and television shows during the 1950s and 1960s, and a real concern to leaders of the military and scientific communities. The United States gathered intelligence through the CIA, FBI, and spy planes, among other tactics, while the Soviet Union employed the infamous KGB and GRU. Throughout the Cold War, direct communication and diplomacy were not always the primary strategies employed by the United States and the Soviet Union. In both countries, leaders changed often due to election cycles and the natural deaths of officeholders. During the first decade of the Cold War, the one in which great strides were made in nuclear weapons technology (in many ways due to spy tactics), Joseph Stalin was the dictator of the Soviet Union. Stalin led the Union of Soviet Socialist Republics from 1929 to 1953, turning it into a military superpower. Though Stalin and his Soviet Union were aligned with the United States and Britain during World War II, Stalin was known, from the start, for his cruel and criminal acts while in office. First appointed by Vladimir Lenin in 1912, Stalin moved up the party ladder at the height of the Communist revolution in Russia, eventually wrestling the control of the Soviet Union into his own hands. In the

Joseph Stalin, leader of the Soviet Union from the mid-1920s to 1953, is shown here with his signature mustache and military uniform.

1920s and 1930s, he ruled with force, sending potential enemies to the gulag, a system of forced labor camps. Those who refused to comply with Stalin's orders were exiled or executed. He also set up collective farms across the country, turning once-private land into huge tracts of farms owned and operated by the state, causing famine and killing a staggering number of citizens.

Joseph Stalin is often cited as a totalitarian ruler, one who required complete subservience. There was no questioning or challenging the dictator, especially with his team of secret police, who had the power to send people to camps or kill them outright. In the late 1930s, Stalin held the Great Purge, a mission to get rid of those who he considered a threat to the Communist Party and Soviet society. His goals of Communist expansion were his first and foremost concerns, above all else, even innocent lives. It is estimated that more than twenty million people were killed under Stalin's rule. He died of a stroke in 1953 and was succeeded by multiple rulers in the years following his death. One of those rulers, Nikita Khrushchev, initiated a de-Stalinization process in order to make the country less repressive. Leading during the height of the Cold War, in the 1960s, Khrushchev reigned with less terror and death, but his actions also caused some of the most tense moments of the war.

Nikita Khrushchev

Nikita Khrushchev was born in Ukraine in 1894, moving to Moscow as a young man and, like Stalin before him, quickly rising through the ranks of the Communist Party.

The KGB

Beginning in the years immediately following Joseph Stalin's rule, the Soviet Union employed a system of secret police, called the Komitet Gosudarstvennoi Bezopanosti (KGB or, in English, the "Committee for State Security"). The KGB was created in 1954 to handle both domestic security and foreign intelligence. It was to serve as the "sword and shield of the Communist Party," protecting the country's security, its political leaders, and its intelligence channels. The KGB were responsible for obtaining the intelligence needed to create advanced submarines, airplanes, and rockets. Over five hundred thousand people worked within the KGB, many of them abroad. After World War II, the organization became the world's largest foreign intelligence service. Inspired by the KGB, American movies, books, and television shows often focused on the popular "secret agent" narrative during the Cold War years.

Though it is often viewed as the counterpart to the Central Intelligence Agency (CIA) in the United States, the KGB performed most of its tasks domestically and against its own citizens. Outside of intelligence gathering, the group, which had over twenty different subgroups or "directorates," provided security of Soviet borders and leaders. The goal of security often bled into pursuit of those who were considered enemies, such as political dissidents, religious activists, human rights activists, and intellectuals. These individuals were harassed, arrested, and sometimes exiled. Though the group has since evolved into the Russian Foreign Intelligence Service and now looks radically different, the KGB were never held accountable for their crimes against the Soviet people, which included imprisonment, harassment, exile, and even death.

Following Stalin's death, Khrushchev became the head of the Party. Though he was once part of Stalin's inner circle, when it came time for Khrushchev's own rule, he spoke out against the former leader, calling for a better relationship with the West and a less oppressive dictatorship. He even traveled to the United States for a peaceful conversation with American leaders. However, tensions between the two countries never fully dissipated, and Khrushchev would later be responsible for stationing nuclear missiles in Cuba, building the Berlin Wall, and allowing great shortages of food in the USSR. In 1964, under pressure from his own party, Khrushchev was forced to resign his position. He died in 1971, after quietly living out the last few years of his life. Following Khrushchev's complicated reign, three other premiers followed: Leonid Brezhnev held the office from 1964 to 1982; Yuri Andropov was in power from 1982 to 1984; and Konstantin Chernenko took the helm for just one year, from 1984 to 1985.

Mikhail Gorbachev

In March 1985, the Soviet Union's last official leader, Mikhail Gorbachev, took office. Though Stalin had set the USSR on a trajectory of continued totalitarian oppression and fear, Gorbachev earned the Nobel Peace Prize in 1990, at the tail end of the Cold War. He worked to democratize the country's political system and resuscitate a Soviet economy that had seen little to no growth in years. He introduced a new policy of *glasnost,* meaning "openness," that allowed for more freedom of expression and information, especially through the media. His political and economic reforms led to an even better relationship with the West, and in 1987 he signed, alongside President Ronald Reagan, the Intermediate-Range Nuclear Forces Treaty, holding both the Soviet Union and the United States accountable for eliminating their intermediate-range nuclear-tipped missiles. It was the first nuclear arms control agreement that reduced nuclear arms. Previous treaties had simply capped the number of arms that could be produced and held. This treaty went a long way toward ending the long-running nuclear arms race between the United States and the USSR.

This photograph, taken by the US Department of Defense in October 1962, shows the medium-range ballistic missile launch site set up by the Soviet Union in San Cristobal, Cuba.

CHAPTER FOUR

Negotiation and Innovation

The decades between 1945 and 1991 were marked by major technological advances, social change, political upheaval, and diplomatic negotiations, in addition to the "cold" threat that loomed over the United States, the Soviet Union, their allies, and their spheres of influence. The two major players regularly antagonized each other through political maneuverings, **propaganda**, proxy wars, and strategically-given economic aid. Throughout this time period, the negotiating table was regularly dominated by boasts about new weapons and, at times, offers of partial disarmament and limited nuclear test bans. As the Cold War heated up and cooled down, going through various stages of tension and relaxation between the two superpowers, the players used both negotiation and innovation to get a "leg up" on the competition, driving themselves further and faster in the arms race and, ultimately, in the war.

Negotiation

One of the first strategies that the United States employed during the Cold War, as we explored in chapter one, was its policy of containment. This policy, first suggested at the end of World War II by George Kennan, a diplomat living in Moscow, sought to contain aggressive Soviet and Communist expansion. The containment period was characterized by **proxy wars** that occurred around the globe. These conflicts often involved the United States intervening in attempts at Communist expansion, be they directly from the Soviet Union or China, or from revolutions within countries themselves. The Korean War is one example of a proxy war. These wars were less about negotiation and more centered on keeping Communism in its place, disallowing states from aligning themselves with that ideology and, tangentially, the USSR.

The Cuban Missile Crisis

One of the most pivotal moments of negotiation occurred on a piece of land removed from both the United States and the Soviet Union—Cuba. On October 22, 1962, President John F. Kennedy made a publicly televised announcement that the Soviet Union had installed nuclear-tipped missiles in Cuba. Up until this moment, both superpowers had been building up their arms to the point of mutually assured destruction. If attacked, the other was sure to attack with full nuclear force, ultimately spelling the end for both countries and, at worst, the world. Over a period of thirteen extremely tense days, President Kennedy and Nikita Khrushchev were locked in a strategic battle over the presence of Soviet missiles at San Cristobal, Cuba. The nuclear weapons, placed there in response to a failed land-attack by the United States, known as the Bay of Pigs Invasion, were meant to dissuade the United States from attempting another attack and overthrowing the country's Communist government. However, they only fired up Kennedy even more, and he

Navy ships, like the aircraft carriers shown here, helped create a blockade around Cuba during the Cuban Missile Crisis in 1962.

consulted his closest advisors to devise a plan of action. Some insisted that another land attack should be attempted; others suggested nothing more than stern warnings. Finally, at the very brink of nuclear war, Kennedy decided to impose a naval "quarantine," or **blockade** that kept military supplies from reaching the country. He announced this decision in a letter to Khrushchev himself. Another tense week of negotiations followed as Soviet ships of offensive weapons were continuously turned away from Cuba by the American blockade. The two countries eventually settled on a deal: the Soviet Union would remove all missiles from Cuba if the United States agreed not to invade. Additionally, the United States would remove all missiles from Turkey within six months. If this offer was rejected, the United States promised to attack Cuba within twenty-four hours. Luckily, in the last moments, Khrushchev accepted the offer, narrowly bringing both countries back from the nuclear precipice they had clung to for two full weeks.

Détente

Following the Cuban Missile Crisis, more productive negotiation tactics began to emerge in the last days of containment and the war in Vietnam. At this time, the United States adopted a new policy of **détente,** from the French word for "relaxation." This period of "cooling" (its start usually dated between 1967 and 1971) was characterized by relaxed tensions between the United States and the Soviet Union. Both countries realized that they were losing out on a positive trade relationship that couldn't exist during tense times. Additionally, the ongoing arms race was becoming more and more expensive, putting strain on the economies of both countries. In May 1972, President Richard Nixon, who was up for reelection and facing scrutiny at home due to the ongoing Vietnam War and strained racial and social tensions, made a historic visit to Moscow, the first president to do so. Nixon and the secretary general of the Communist Party, Leonid Brezhnev, signed seven agreements during their visit, covering topics ranging from cooperative research to expanded trade to arms control.

The negotiations weren't just limited to the two countries; in 1975, thirty-five nations came together to sign the Helsinki Final Act, concluding the Conference on Security and Cooperation in Europe. The act, signed after two years of the conference, addressed multiple global issues, including trade, human rights, politics, and military concerns. Though the act formally accepted Soviet annexation of several countries (a result of Soviet expansionism), it also cemented certain human rights protections that improved the lives of activists and dissidents in Europe. In general, greater cooperation was forged between Eastern and Western Europe as a result of the Helsinki Final Act and follow-up conferences, indirectly aiding in the continued détente and, eventually, helping to bring an end to Soviet domination and the Cold War.

Toward the end of the 1970s, the détente began to break down. Proxy wars and military interventions had continued, and the competition for military dominance between the United States and Soviet Union did not seem to be slowing as much as the public had expected. In 1979, the Soviet Union invaded Afghanistan, stalling SALT II and ending arms control talks for the near future. In 1980, the United

States boycotted the summer Olympics, set to be held in Moscow. Jimmy Carter, president at the time, reacted to the invasion of Afghanistan by boosting the defense budget and sending financial aid to Pakistan, where political leaders were subsidizing anti-Soviet efforts. The 1980 election cemented the end of détente with the election of Ronald Reagan, who ran on an anti-détente platform and emphasized the necessity of strength in peacekeeping.

Innovation

The Cold War years, in addition to being a time of tension and negotiation, were also marked by great advances in

President Richard M. Nixon and Soviet leader Leonid Brezhnev sign the SALT I treaty in May, 1972.

technology, weaponry, and education. We have seen the ways in which nuclear technology made huge strides at the end of World War II and into the first years of the Cold War, introducing the world to the A-bomb, hydrogen bomb, nuclear-tipped missiles, and defensive weapons that could destroy attempts at offensive nuclear bomb drops. Throughout the 1940s, 1950s, and 1960s, new submarine technology, communication satellites, and medical devices were introduced. Both the United States and the Soviet Union grew more adept at running their militaries using new technology while at the same time ramping up consumer technology, such as cable television (1948), the barcode (1952), the laser (1960), and the measles vaccine (1964). None of these innovations were created in a vacuum. They were all the result of the international relations and domestic policies at play during the years directly following World War II.

Sputnik

During World War II, the United States remained sure of its dominance in all things related to science, technology, and industry. Coming out of the war as victors, the United States enjoyed a time of prosperity, pride, national security and enhanced quality of life for many citizens. America had been the first to create and use the atomic bomb, and even with the Soviets' nuclear advancements, Americans remained sure of their technological superiority. This notion changed, however, with the launch of *Sputnik* on October 4, 1957. The world's first artificial **satellite,** or orbiting object, sent the world hurling into the "space age" and caused many in the United States to question American dominance on the

The Red Telephone

Following the Cuban Missile Crisis, wherein messages from President Kennedy and Nikita Khrushchev were written down and took nearly a day to reach their destination, the two sides decided that they needed an easier and faster way to reach each other, especially during a tense time in which millions of lives were at stake. In June 1963, the United States and the Soviet Union formally agreed to establish direct communication for use in times of emergency. Popular culture soon picked up on the idea, and the myth of the "red telephone" was born. Featured in movies like *Fail-Safe* and television shows like *Batman*, the red phone became a mainstay in the popular imagination. It was also featured in *Get Smart* and even more recently in *The West Wing*. For decades now, the image of a bright red phone that connected the oval office to the Soviet Union has remained embedded in the minds of Americans.

This is one myth, though, that is easily debunked. There was never a red telephone at all. There were, instead, teletype machines installed in the Kremlin and in the Pentagon, which is the actual home of the hotline—not the White House. There are also encoding devices in both locations to help with language translation. The hotline began operation in August 1963, just three months before the assassination of John F. Kennedy, who never typed out a telegram on the machine. President Lyndon Johnson was the first to use it in communications with Alexei Kosygin during the Six-Day War between Israel and the neighboring countries of Egypt, Jordan, and Syria. In 1971, the hotline was updated with a satellite connection, and in the 1980s, it gained high-speed fax capabilities, soon rendering the teletype link unnecessary. A fiber-optic link for email and talking was installed in 2008.

Sputnik 1, the first artificial Earth satellite, was launched by the Soviets in 1957. The polished metal sphere had four external radio antennae.

world stage. *Sputnik*, a 184 pound (83.5 kilogram), 22-inch (0.6 meter) round item with four long, silver antennae, circled Earth once every hour and twenty-six minutes. Those with radio skills could pick up its beeps on the dial, hearing the tinny sound as it passed over America several times a day. The satellite could also be seen with binoculars in the early dawn, a visual reminder of this newfound Soviet superiority that had caught so many American scientists, politicians, and military leaders off-guard and struck fear into their hearts, as the technology could potentially be used in a threatening manner. Taking it to the next level, the Soviets launched, on November 3 of that same year, *Sputnik 2*. Inside its more conical body, this advanced satellite even held a live dog!

The American people, and especially the American government, were not pleased with the way the space race was playing out. On January 31, 1958, the first United States satellite, *Explorer*, was launched. The race would continue throughout the next decade with even more satellites, people in space, and orbits around the moon, culminating with the American-manned lunar landing in 1969. The launch of *Sputnik*, however, didn't just affect the United States' relationship with space advancements. It also helped to propel the country onto a trajectory of science education, research, and development that, to this day, has not slowed down. In the months after the Soviet launch of *Sputnik*, it became clear to the American people that education in the USSR was the key to the steps they'd taken to get ahead in both the space race and arms race. Soon, great support grew for a stronger federal role in American education, especially at the university level. These voices, combined with critics of the school systems, then governed for the most part by the states, allowed for a major turn in the education of young adults.

Education

Following World War II, the G.I. Bill of Rights, put in place by President Franklin D. Roosevelt, allowed for the reabsorption of veterans returning from overseas. The bill helped thousands of veterans attend universities and receive

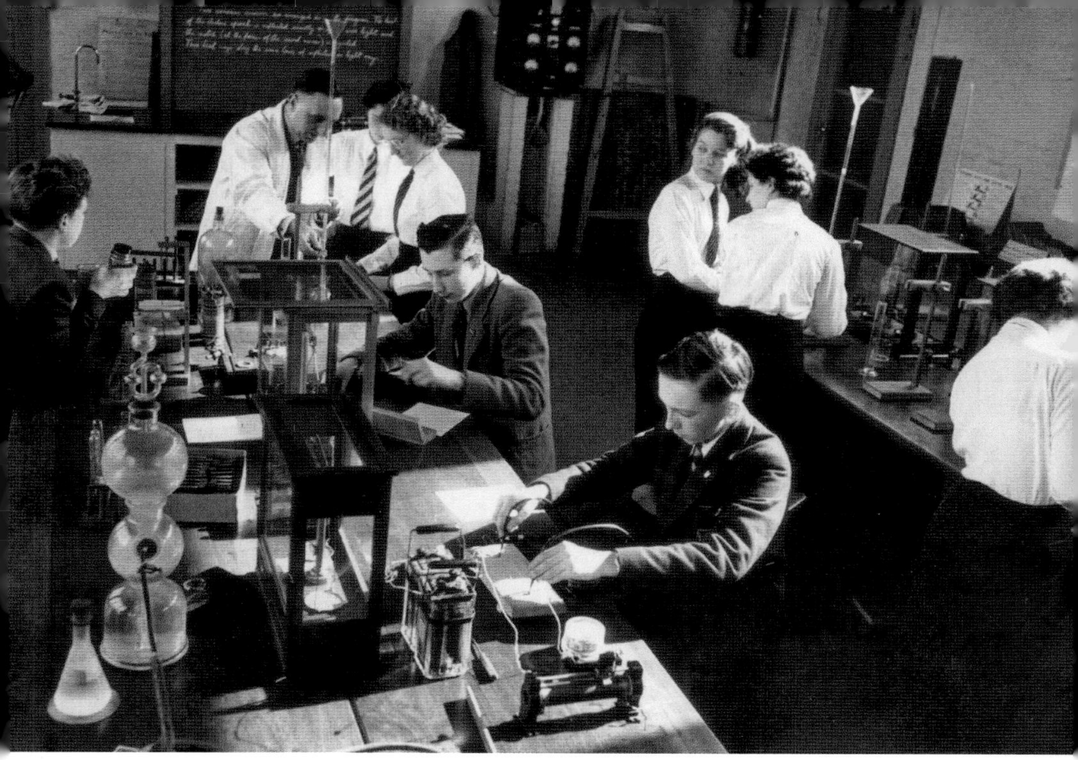

Following World War II, the federal government began to invest heavily in science education.

higher education, and those colleges churned out scientists, engineers, and others in technological fields that could help with defense efforts. After the launch of *Sputnik*, federal investment in colleges and universities grew to a massive scale, and the public was convinced of the need for more improved higher education in order to beat the Soviet Union in the multiple "races" that were now running between the two superpowers. From elementary school to the college level, the federal government began to invest in the education of future scientists and engineers while also heavily funding research universities. Though the United States could not and would not move toward a centralized system, instead keeping most control of education at the state and local levels, there was a massive shift towards more oversight of state-run

Propaganda

Very few periods of history, in the United States and across the globe, have not been marked by the widespread use of propaganda—information, often biased or misleading, that is used to promote a certain political cause or point of view. The Cold War, as much a war of ideologies as one of military superiority, featured propaganda on both sides of the ocean: American media demonized Communism while the Soviet government persuaded its people that capitalism and democracy would be the downfall of the United States and the world. In the early years of the war, propaganda was explicit and clear, while in later years it became more subtle, driven by psychology and consumer behavior. Examples of classic vehicles for propaganda included direct or indirect messaging in films, television shows, newspapers, posters, educational materials, and even candy wrappers. Print, audio, and video propaganda used rich imagery and inflammatory language to tug at viewers' emotions and sway them to support one side or the other.

In the United States, many television shows and movies in the 1940s and 1950s revolved around the positive attributes of living in a capitalist, consumer-driven society and the dangers of spies and secret agents. Additionally, clear anti-Communist messages were delivered through newspaper articles, posters, and patriotic films. In American and Soviet schools, children were heavily targeted as accessible consumers of political messaging. Educational videos, youth organizations, and nuclear attack drills became part of everyday life for children going to school during the Cold War years. The countries' respective governments hoped that constant messaging would convince citizens that one ideology was better than the other and that they were, more importantly, worth fighting for.

systems, more funding for the most promising students, more collection of data, and the promotion of science curricula.

The National Defense of Education Act, signed in 1958, clearly stated, "an educational emergency exists and requires action by the federal government. Assistance will come from Washington to help develop as rapidly as possible those skills essential to the national security." Suddenly, federal educational expenditures more than doubled. Federal student loans, aid for teacher education, graduate fellowships in science and engineering, research and development at universities, and elementary-level curriculum development all received significant boosts from the Act. Foreign languages, science, and math were the cornerstones of a document that has changed American education in numerous ways. The desire for increased science, technology, engineering, and math (STEM) educational efforts has only gained force, catapulting STEM initiatives into the forefront of the American experience. During the Cold War, these initiatives helped to change the direction of the war itself, increasing the American opportunity for technological advancements, especially related to military and defense. It also provided the military-industrial complex with intellectual fodder that would carry on for generations, informing not only output in terms of ideas and innovations, but radically shifting American values around the purpose and promise of American education as a tool for growth. The Cold War brought education out of the personal and into the political, shaping its purpose and directing its structure for decades to come.

During a celebration in New Delhi, India, a ballistic missile is paraded through the streets. Throughout the past few decades, development and acquisition of nuclear weapons has continued to spread across the world.

CHAPTER FIVE

The Legacy of Nuclear Proliferation, the Military-Industrial Complex, and the Arms Race

Without the advent of the nuclear age, the Cold War may have taken a very different course. In fact, without deadly nuclear weapons, the war may never have happened at all. When Einstein wrote to President Truman in 1939, warning him of the potential for a Soviet-made fission weapon, he certainly did not imagine the years of tension, conflict, and arms buildup. Nor could he foresee the pain, death, major industrial and economic changes, and proliferation of nuclear weapons that would occur following the successful creation by the United States of that first destructive weapon. Had he known this, Einstein may have foregone his letter, or penned a more careful note, or worked to shut down the building of such a bomb. Unfortunately, it seems as though we may never know a world without the potential for nuclear war, even in recent decades that are less marked by constant threat. The successful test and use of the first fission atomic bomb caused more than a nuclear reaction—it set off a chain of events that would lead to a competitive weapons marketplace, the creation of more destructive nuclear weapons, and the evolution of the United States economy into one that is thoroughly influenced and partially driven by demand for plentiful, military-grade weapons and materials.

Nuclear Proliferation

In the 1970s, 1980s, and 1990s, nuclear weapons programs were moving in two distinctly different streams. On one hand, the United States and the Soviet Union negotiated several treaties and documents that limited the growth of arsenals, restricted ballistic missile use, and put controls on which countries could develop nuclear weapons or peaceful nuclear energy. In the 1990s especially, the United States and the Soviet Union became less focused on their own weapons stockpiles (though they would continue, through the present day, to build up arsenals) and became more focused on nuclear weapons in other parts of the world. While disarmament talks were occurring between the Americans and Soviets, other countries began their own nuclear weapon research and manufacture programs. More information had become available, especially after the United States entered the Internet age, and materials also became easier to come by. Though the Nuclear Non-Proliferation Treaty is now the most widely accepted arms control agreement, with nearly all members of the United Nation signing on, three countries—Israel, India, and Pakistan—refused to sign the document. One country, North Korea, recently threatened to withdraw from the Treaty altogether. Israel does not admit to possessing nuclear weapons, and, as far as we know, has not tested any weapons. Its close neighbor and historical adversary, Pakistan, conducted its first successful nuclear weapon test in 1998. As they are not signers of the NPT, Pakistan is not in violation of the Treaty. However, countries can still make sanctions against it by placing new taxes on

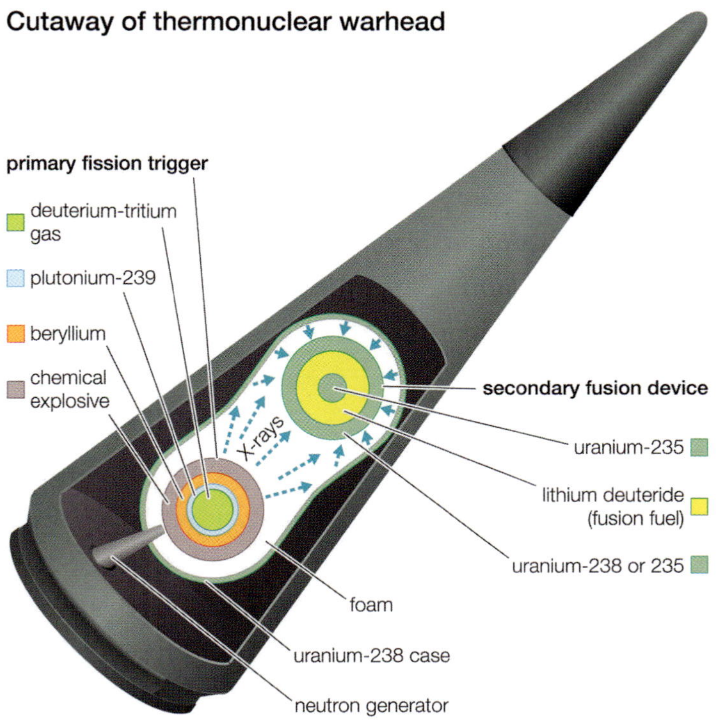

This diagram displays the inner workings of a nuclear warhead.

imports, disallowing imports altogether, and refusing to buy Pakistan's exports. Many would argue that it is in Pakistan's best interest to cease any nuclear tests or attempts to construct nuclear weapons. However, some countries believe that it is in the interest of their safety, that they need this type of weapon to defend themselves from outside threats, or that they need these weapons in order to make clear that they should not be threatened. This position harkens back to the United States policy of deterrence—letting others know that a country can retaliate, causing other nations to hold back from potential offensive maneuvers or land grabs.

In the mid-1990s, Middle Eastern countries such as Iraq and Iran began searching for nuclear weapon information and materials. Today, global fears have shifted away from a nuclear war between the United States and Russia and turned to threats of terrorism around the world. There are ideological, religious, and political battles being fought on many fronts, and it has become easier to produce and transport nuclear weapons of a more manageable size. Some fear that "radiological dispersive devices" (RDDs), or "dirty bombs," could become the newest weapon of choice for terrorist organizations. RDDs combine conventional explosives with radioactive material, strategically dispersing radiation in crowded areas. The amount of radiation in a dirty bomb, perhaps connected to dynamite and thrown into a public space, could make people sick, cause cancer, and contaminate the facility in which it is thrown. The United States Nuclear Regulatory Commission has stated that terrorist arrests and prosecutions overseas have revealed that "individuals associated with al-Qaeda planned to acquire materials for a RDD." Though none of these dirty bombs have been found or used yet, we must remain aware of all potential nuclear threats, however relatively small they may be, because radiation can have such a devastating and lasting impact on a given area and population.

In July 2016, the Arms Control Association reported that, though President Obama did not make progress on nuclear disarmament during his second term in office, he did take steps to improve nuclear materials security. In 2015, the Obama administration headed up the Iran Nuclear Deal, an agreement that included Iran's promise to repurpose one of its uranium plants into a science center while it cuts back on uranium production at its sister facility. It also agreed to redesign and rebuild its nuclear reactor in order to prevent it from producing weapons-grade plutonium. Going forward, the International Atomic Energy Agency will have greater access to Iran's nuclear program. If Iran follows the points outlined in the agreement, it will receive relief from arms sanctions. These penalties have cut Iran off from importing (non-nuclear) arms and missiles from the United States.

The Arms Race

The arms race of the Cold War era, though it has cooled, rewarmed, and changed course many times over the last seven decades, is still being run. In the last years of the Cold War, the players found themselves in an all-out sprint. During the last two years of the war, when President Reagan

President Ronald Reagan and Secretary Mikhail Gorbachev sign the Intermediate-Range Nuclear Forces Treaty in 1987, an agreement requiring that both parties destroy certain types of missiles.

was in office, the United States spent over two trillion dollars to build up both conventional and nuclear forces. Bombers, ICBMs, submarine missiles, and navy ships were all put into increased production. The Strategic Defense Initiative (SDI), announced in 1983, which would come to be known by its nickname, "Star Wars," was an expensive plan to launch weapons into space that could destroy enemy missiles midflight. The plan was in direct violation of several United States and Soviet agreements that had pushed for disarmament progress over the years. While critics worried that the SDI was, ultimately, an ineffective plan that would unnecessarily speed up the arms race, Reagan championed it as a way to destroy the Russian economy. If Russia was busy producing missiles in order to compete, its economy would be badly strained. However, evidence does not show that the Soviets, in response to the SDI, did much to increase defense spending.

The United States budget deficit, on the other hand, continued to balloon, due in no small part to the rise in military expenditures as United States initiatives and arms buildup dominated the first half of the 1980s. As Mikhail Gorbachev came into power in 1985, the Soviet Union came to dominate the end of the Cold War. Gorbachev came to believe that arms control was essential to the end of the Cold War and the return of a stable economy in the Soviet Union. Arms talks resumed between the United States and the Soviets, resulting in the Intermediate Nuclear Forces Treaty, or INF. This was the first arms *reduction,* rather than simply an arms limitation, of the Cold War. Both the United

States and the Soviet Union reduced their arms as a result of the INF. In the following months and years, Gorbachev continued to make cutbacks on Soviet arms, moving to a position of defensive preparedness in the event of an attack, rather than an all-out offensive arms position.

While both the United States and Russia began to slow down their respective buildups of nuclear and conventional

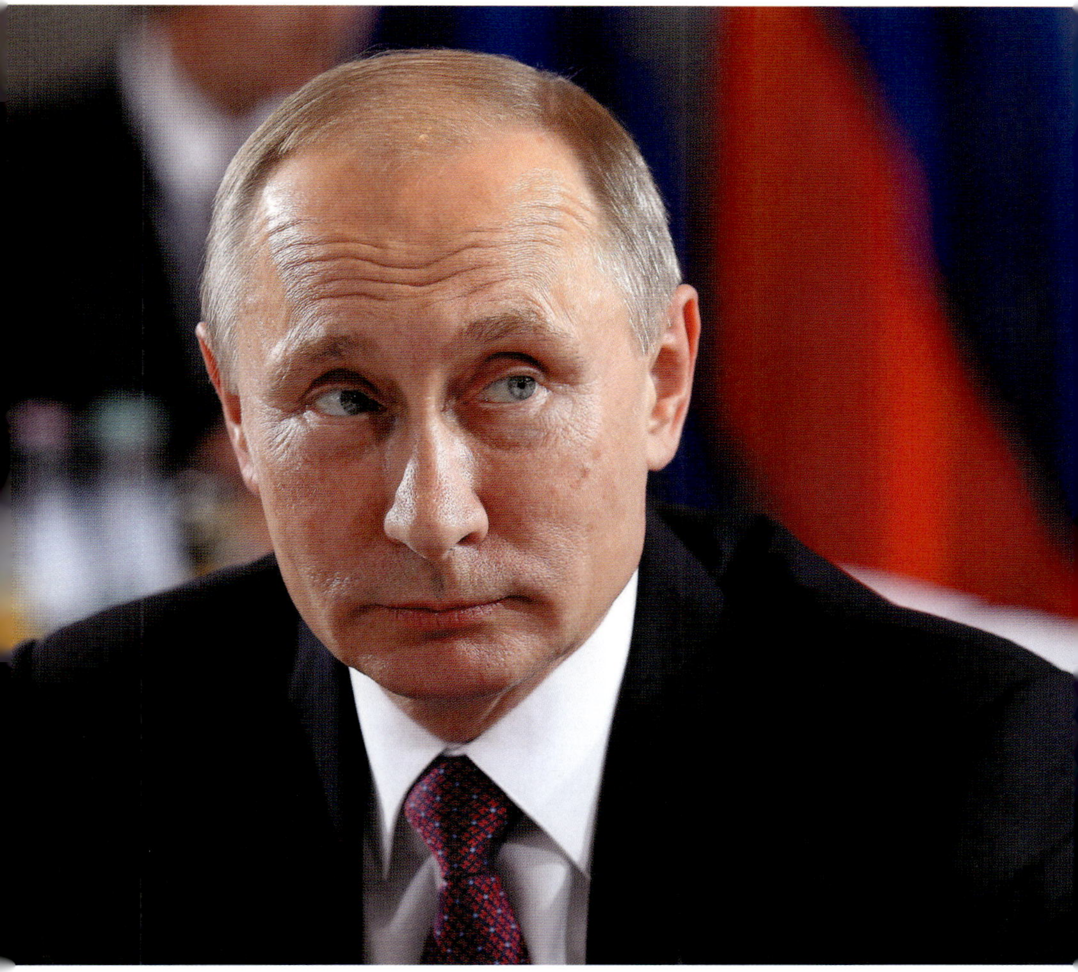

Vladimir Putin is the current president of the Russian Federation and has held office since 2012.

weapons in the later years of the Cold War, the current climate around arms could not be easily described as "sparse" or "reduced." Recent reports by the Arms Control Association note that the United States is devoting large amounts of resources to maintain and upgrade nuclear weapons delivery systems and warheads. American nuclear weapons, positioned in strategic locations around the world, are poised and ready to fire should the United States or one of its allies be attacked. The report, which grades eleven key countries, found that states possessing nuclear weapons demonstrated "little to no progress" in reduction of their forces. Russia has recently rejected proposals for nuclear reductions, instead taking steps to develop a new ground-launched cruise missile. Moscow also increased its number of deployed warheads to levels that exceeded treaty limits; Russia has until 2018 to bring its numbers back down or face further sanctions. Russia also opted out of the 2016 Nuclear Security Summit and no longer participates in the Global Partnership Against the Spread of Weapons of Mass Destruction.

Though relations between Russia and the United States have not reached the levels of tension experienced during the Cold War, the two countries remain nuclear superpowers and, if conflicts ever arose, would be able to attack or defend themselves quickly and decisively.

Military-Industrial Complex

When President Dwight D. Eisenhower warned the country, in 1961, of what he termed the "military-industrial complex,"

The Business of Defense

Nuclear weapons, the arms race, and the military-industrial complex were all created in response to a perceived threat, be it the threat of nuclear war, the threat of Communism, or one of many other real and urgent worries that coalesced during the first years of World War II. In the Communist Soviet Union, the business of producing weapons, just like the business of producing lamps, food, and other consumer products, was a collective one, and was led by the government itself. In the United States, on the other hand, weapons research and production, though they may be under the distant direction of the government, are ultimately left to the private sector. In the American capitalist system, defense companies form contracts with the government that allow them to produce weapons and technology in return for government dollars. The military, weapons contractors, and Congress work together to form a web or, as Eisenhower put it, a *complex* that has the power to lobby for higher levels of military spending than we might actually need.

This complicated system becomes muddied even further when one considers that defense contractors often finance think tanks that help influence policies—military spending policies—that then can benefit the companies themselves. This means that a company that builds warships, missiles, and nuclear technology may also be influencing Congress to take military action in other parts of the globe and extend our current reach even deeper, necessitating more weapons.

he spoke with concern and urgency, though he could not have imagined the United States of today—one in which defense spending dwarfs that of every other country, topping out at nearly six billion dollars in 2015, according to the International Institute for Strategic Studies and its Military Balance 2016 report. This year, the United States accounts for more than a third of global spending on defense and that number shows no signs of shrinking. The military-industrial complex as we know it today got its start even before Pearl Harbor, as the United States readied itself defensively at the end of World War II. The idea truly came to dominate the particular brand of United States capitalism during the Cold War, years in which more destructive weapons were created and deployed at staggering rates. The "permanent armaments industry" that Eisenhower imagined had emerged, combining a huge military establishment and a large arms industry, ultimately blurring the lines between the public and private sectors to produce an all-encompassing ecosystem that feeds not only the United States military, but militaries around the world.

In 2010, the United States exported "major conventional weapons" to sixty-two countries. These ranged from combat jets to helicopters, tanks, and guided missiles. Defense contractors (the companies that enter into contracts to produce weapons and gear for the military) applaud the expansion of the "complex," as it gives them a steady stream of work and they can therefore supply jobs to those who need work. Congress often readily supports these defense contracts, which provide jobs in their districts. It is this last piece of the puzzle, the Congress, that turns Eisenhower's

The United States armed forces, currently operating in over one hundred countries, has the world's largest military budget.

military-industrial complex into the military-industrial-congressional complex, a phrase that has been falsely attributed to Eisenhower speechwriters and prior versions of his speech over the years. However, no evidence exists to back up that claim. The phrase, though, remains, as do the structures and relationships that embroil the United States in weapons trading on an immense scale.

Though the world weathered a decline in global arms sales in 2010 due to the Great Recession, the United States has kept at it, selling tens of billions of dollars worth of arms to foreign countries each and every year. Similarly, Russia remains a large producer and exporter of arms, second only to the United States. All told, the proliferation of destructive nuclear weapons across the globe has fueled an ever-expanding arms race, cementing the military-industrial complex, both in the United States, Russia, and elsewhere, as the dominant system at play. In order to continue supplying jobs, weapons must always be made, and countries (whether in conflict or at peace) must always be in need of those materials. That system, its place solidified during the decades following World War II, will remain in place for the foreseeable future, unless some extremely significant changes are made.

The same can be said of nuclear proliferation and the arms race—though the path may have changed course, the existence of powerful, destructive nuclear weapons and the drive to create bigger, better weapons technology will remain a part of our global existence unless a major ideological change occurs. This is why the study of history, and the knowledge of the Cold War in particular, in addition to the oft-studied wars, is so incredibly important. What we learn from the actions of governments, diplomats, and military leaders of the past will affect our actions today and into the future. We get to decide if nuclear weapons will be kept and deployed in our countries. We get to make choices about who we elect to lead our militaries and order our weapons production. And we get to decide, no matter what country we live in or which political system we support, if we truly value global peace. If we do believe in global peace, then we get to choose how we will live out that value every day.

Chronology

1939 Albert Einstein writes to President Truman, warning of the potential for a Soviet-made nuclear weapon.

1941 The Manhattan Project, a secret American effort to create a nuclear weapon, is born.

1945 The United States drops atomic bombs on Hiroshima and Nagasaki. World War II ends.

1949 NATO is formed. The Soviet Union conducts a successful test of its own atomic bomb.

1952 The hydrogen bomb is tested in the United States; the United Kingdom tests an independently developed nuclear weapon.

1953 Joseph Stalin dies. Dwight D. Eisenhower is elected president of the United States.

1955 The Warsaw Pact is signed.

1957 *Sputnik* is launched.

1961 President Eisenhower warns of the military-industrial complex in his farewell address.

1962 The Cuban Missile Crisis occurs, marking the high point of tension in the Cold War.

1963	The United States and Soviet Union formally agree to establish a hotline between the two countries; the Limited Test Ban Treaty is signed.
1964	China becomes a nuclear power.
1968	The Nuclear Non-Proliferation Treaty is signed.
1972	President Nixon makes an historical trip to Moscow to meet with General Secretary Leonid Brezhnev.
1979	The Soviet Union invades Afghanistan, ending arms control talks for the near future.
1980	Ronald Reagan is elected president, formally ending the period of détente.
1987	Mikhail Gorbachev and President Ronald Reagan sign the Intermediate-Range Nuclear Forces Treaty, eliminating all short and mid-range missiles and launchers.
1989	The Berlin Wall comes down, marking an ease in Berlin's relations with the West.
1991	The Strategic Arms Reduction Treaty is signed but doesn't go into effect until 2001.
1998	Pakistan conducts its first successful nuclear test.

Glossary

annex To add an area of land to one's own territory, usually by seizure of someone else's land.

arms race A competition between two or more parties for superiority in the production and accumulation of weapons and armies.

arsenal A collection of weapons or place of storage for weapons.

blockade The act of physically sealing off a space and disallowing the entry of goods or people.

capitalism An economic system based on private control of a free market; goods that are used to make and transport products are owned by individuals instead of governments.

Communism An economic system based on communal control; goods that are used to make and transport products are owned by the "commons" or the government.

containment The policy of preventing the spread of an influence, ideology, or country.

détente The release of tension or hostility, especially between nations, often marked by negotiations or agreement.

deterrence The threat of retaliation to ward off an enemy attack.

diplomacy The skill or profession of managing international relations and negotiations.

espionage The practice of using spies, often to obtain confidential information.

intercontinental ballistic missile (ICBM) A guided missile, capable of traveling over 3,400 miles (5,472 kilometers), that is designed to deliver a nuclear warhead to a predetermined location.

iron curtain The name, given by Winston Churchill, for the boundary that divided Europe into two distinct areas during the Cold War.

Manhattan Project An American research and development initiative that resulted in the creation of the first nuclear weapons.

mutually assured destruction (MAD) The idea that full-scale use of nuclear weapons would cause destruction of both the attacker and the targeted country.

NATO The North Atlantic Treaty Organization is a military alliance, created in 1949, that holds signers responsible for collective defense in the event that another member is attacked.

nuclear fission The splitting of the nucleus of an atom into smaller parts, creating a very large release of energy.

proliferation A rapid growth or increase.

propaganda Information or statements, often misleading, biased, or false, that are used to help or harm a specific cause, person, group, movement, or point of view.

satellite An artificial object or machine that has been put into orbit.

Bibliography

Broad, William J., and Sergio Peçanha. "The Iran Nuclear Deal–A Simple Guide." *The New York Times*, January 15, 2015. http://www.nytimes.com/interactive/2015/03/31/world/middleeast/simple-guide-nuclear-talks-iran-us.html?_r=1.

Edwards, Lee, and Elizabeth Edwards Spalding. *A Brief History of the Cold War*. Washington, DC: Regency History, 2016.

Freedman, Lawrence. *The Cold War*. London: Cassell & Co., 2001.

Isaacs, Jeremy, and Taylor Downing. *Cold War: An Illustrated History, 1945–1991*. Boston: Little, Brown and Company, 1998.

Jogalekar, Ashton. "The Many Tragedies of Edward Teller." *Scientific American*, January 2014. http://blogs.scientificamerican.com/the-curious-wavefunction/the-many-tragedies-of-edward-teller/.

Ledbetter, James. *Unwarranted Influence: Dwight D. Eisenhower and the Military-Industrial Complex*. New Haven: Yale University Press, 2011.

Pace, Eric. "Klaus Fuchs, Physicist Who Gave Atom Secrets to Soviet, Dies at 76." *The New York Times*,

January 1988. http://www.nytimes.com/1988/01/29/obituaries/klaus-fuchs-physicist-who-gave-atom-secrets-to-soviet-dies-at-76.html.

Painter, David S. *The Cold War: An International History.* New York: Routledge, 1999.

Philipp, Elizabeth, and Kelsey Davenport. "Assessing Progress on Nuclear Nonproliferation and Disarmament: Updated Report Card 2013–2016." *Arms Control Association,* July 2016. http://www.armscontrol.org/files/2016_ReportCard_reduced.pdf.

Rosen, Rebecca J. "Technology Mythology: No Red Phone Ever Connected the White House and Moscow." *The Atlantic,* June 26, 2013. http://www.theatlantic.com/technology/archive/2013/06/technology-mythology-no-red-phone-ever-connected-the-white-house-to-moscow/277259/.

Taylor, Adam, and Laris Karklis. "This Remarkable Chart Shows How U.S. Defense Spending Dwarfs the Rest of the World." *The Washington Post,* February 2016. http://www.washingtonpost.com/news/worldviews/wp/2016/02/09/this-remarkable-chart-shows-how-u-s-defense-spending-dwarfs-the-rest-of-the-world/.

Wolly, Brian. "Eisenhower's Farewell Speech, 50 Years Later." *Smithsonian.com,* January 14, 2011. http://www.smithsonianmag.com/smithsonian-institution/eisenhowers-farewell-speech-50-years-later-4356528/?no-ist.

Further Information

Books

Engle, Margarita. *Enchanted Air: Two Cultures, Two Wings: A Memoir.* New York: Atheneum Books for Young Readers, 2016.

Goldsmith, Connie. *Bombs Over Bikini: The World's First Nuclear Disaster.* Minneapolis: Twenty-First Century Books, 2014.

Orr, Tamra B. *The Atom Bomb: Creating and Exploding the First Nuclear Weapon.* New York: Rosen Publishing Group, 2005.

Roxburgh, Ellis. *John F. Kennedy vs. Nikita Khrushchev: Cold War Adversaries (History's Greatest Rivals).* New York City: Gareth Stevens Publishing, 2015.

Websites

Cold War International History Project

http://www.wilsoncenter.org/program/cold-war-international-history-project

The Cold War International History Project is a comprehensive resource for any and all information about the Cold War, especially perspectives from the non-Western world.

Federation of American Scientists: Status of World Nuclear Forces

http://fas.org/issues/nuclear-weapons/status-world-nuclear-forces/

This website displays in detail each country's inventory of nuclear warheads from 1945 to 2016.

PBS: American Experience

http://www.pbs.org/wgbh/amex/bomb/maps/index.html

The "Race for the Superbomb" website provides a map of all official nuclear tests that have occurred since the dawn of the nuclear weapons age.

Voices of the Manhattan Project

http://manhattanprojectvoices.org/

This joint project by the Atomic Heritage Foundation and the Los Alamos Historical Society is a public archive of oral history collections of Manhattan Project veterans and their families, and it features four hundred audio and visual interviews with workers and their families.

Videos

Eisenhower Farewell Address

http://www.youtube.com/watch?v=CWiIYW_fBfY

This is a full video of President Dwight D. Eisenhower's farewell address to the nation, given in 1961.

Unedited Footage of the Bombing of Nagasaki

http://www.youtube.com/watch?v=Z9v5sW6t0zI

This unedited footage shows the detonation of the atomic bomb on Nagasaki.

Index

Page numbers in **boldface** are illustrations. Entries in **boldface** are glossary terms.

About the Author

Kaitlyn Duling believes in the power of words to change hearts, minds, and, ultimately, actions. A poet, nonfiction author, and grant writer who grew up in Illinois, she now resides in Pittsburgh, Pennsylvania, where she works aboard a bookmobile and helps kids learn to love to read. She knows that knowledge of the past is the key to our future and wants to make sure that all children and families have access to high-quality information. This is her second book for Cavendish Square Publishing.